Preface

This poem hangs on the inside wall just next to the front door of our home:

YES, YES, YOU CAN

Frogs, vultures, beetles, and rocks,
All kinds of people in all kinds of flocks;
They all share some things together,
A hope, a dream, a reason, a scheme.

In your life you'll know them all.
Hitch your dreams to a star; follow them big or small;
But remember we're united by a painful blow
That comes when the world hisses its heartless NO!

When you admit your dreams so large,
People will say you're a dunce and a fool by far;
They're hopeless and jealous, beating you is their plan.
Stand defiant and cocksure and thunder, "I CAN!"

"No way," your friends say, they'll cackle and spit,
The hopes in your heart they carelessly miss.
But feed those dreams, keep them healthy and large,
Ignore the naysayers and yell simply, "CHARGE!"

Those needling, lifeless skeptics abound,
Circling like buzzards, your schemes to tear down;
But fan the fire that you feel inside.
Take wings of eagles and proclaim, "STEP ASIDE!"

Life has enemies that will test your mettle,
Make you strong, though you'll feel no better;
Nothing will be easy or delivered on a plate.
If you don't do yourself, you always just wait.

My prayers for you sound like, "Father, ignite them!
Though the odds are steep, let Your presence excite them."
A special reply will embolden your wit;
Remember in tired moments, it don't pay to quit!

May the music of victory sound sweet in your ear.
Run quickly! Hustle swiftly! Now the goal is near!
What will distinguish your magic is how much you care,
Not muscle, not brawn, only what you dare.

Though the cynics' arrows may find their mark,
Pierce your resolve and break your heart;
When you lay bleeding along life's road,
Then you must remember what you've hereby been told.

Never with more love did a person God make,
Than you, your strengths and weaknesses consummate;
He'll be there when you're broken, shaken, and tattered,
Directing you to think on those things that matter.

Through bitter tears you'll wonder if you can,
But ignore your fears and make a dazzling plan.

BOYS!

WILLIAM BEAUSAY II

OLIVER
NELSON
™

THOMAS NELSON PUBLISHERS®
Nashville

A Division of Thomas Nelson, Inc.
www.ThomasNelson.com

Published in Nashville, Tennessee, by Thomas Nelson, Inc.

Excerpt from CONCEPTUAL BLOCKBUSTING by James L. Adams. Copyright © 1974 by James L. Adams. Reprinted with permission of W. H. Freeman and Company.

The Bible version used in this publication is THE NEW KING JAMES VERSION. Copyright © 1979, 1980, 1982, Thomas Nelson, Inc., Publishers.

Library of Congress Cataloging-in-Publication Data

Beausay, William, 1957–
    Boys! / William Beausay II.
        p. cm.
    ISBN 0-7852-6528-7
    1. Boys. 2. Child Rearing. I. Title.
HQ775.B38 1994
649'.132—dc20

93–48889
CIP

Printed in the United States of America
02 03 04 05 06 PHX 27 26 25 24 23

Contents

From your dreams naysayers shall ever be banned,

And hear me gently whispering in your ear,

"Yes, yes, you can!"

It's my "Parent's Pledge." I wrote it originally for my kids, and each morning as they headed out to start a new day, I reminded them to just say yes: "The world is going to take its big boot and try to step right in your face. Don't let 'em beat you!" I believe in setting the mental switches on "Go!" and unplugging defeat before it starts each morning.

I love kids, and I want them all to be winners. However, I'm painfully aware of the improbable nature of my vision, and I confess a grinding sadness about it. For all my life I have felt a deep admiration for children who are winners, and a special fondness and caring for children who—for whatever reason—are not. My destiny is to do something on behalf of all kids and to do my part to raise all children to higher levels.

I set before myself a goal to write a book that *I'd* never seen. I was so tired of reading child development books that left me asking myself, *So what do I do now?* You've no doubt found yourself asking the same maddening question, panning in the river of great ideas to find some nuggets you can spend. *What's needed,* I thought, *is something fresh and forceful.*

I want your son to be glad you read this book, and I want your boy to feel lucky to have you as a parent. For that, you need to have some tools that can be sensibly applied to raising a winner. The tools need to be simple and logical, meshing easily with natural parental urges and instincts. Apply them properly, and you can know the feeling of winning at the most crucial job in your busy life.

I firmly believe in the radical nature of the idea tools you are about to consider. I also believe that if your attitude is proper, you cannot possibly fail to raise a winner. What's proper? Optimistic to a fault, stridently patient, obnoxiously hardheaded, and brimming with love. These are the precursors to parental excellence. Follow them and I can confidently assure your entry into a new realm of child-rearing effectiveness!

Above all else, I admonish you to gain wisdom. King Solomon recited some teaching on wisdom he received as a boy:

> When I was my father's son,
> Tender and the only one in the sight of my mother,
> He also taught me, and said to me:
> "Let your heart retain my words;
> Keep my commands, and live.
> Get wisdom! Get understanding!
> Do not forget, nor turn away from the words of my mouth.
> Do not forsake her, and she will preserve you;
> Love her, and she will keep you.
> Wisdom is the principal thing;
> Therefore get wisdom.
> And in all your getting, get understanding.
> Exalt her, and she will promote you;
> She will bring you honor, when you embrace her.
> She will place on your head an ornament of grace;
> A crown of glory she will deliver to you." (Prov. 4:3–9)

And you thought parental speeches were ignored! This book will provide many ways for you to begin the exciting journey of creating a son who is remarkable by any standard. Apply yourself diligently, and look for wisdom and understanding. When you feel yourself slipping or failing or wandering about in frustrated ignorance, you will hear me gently whispering in your ear, "Yes, yes, you can."

CHAPTER 1

Dear Mom and Dad . . .

 Raising winning boys starts with keeping an open mind and considering many interesting parameters. Here are some ideas for both parents.

I NEED TO THROW A PITCH I KNOW YOU'LL SWING FOR

Quite a few years ago I conducted the first of my "Raising Winners" seminars. I had recently descended from the perch of my academic tower, and I wasn't prepared for the dirt I was going to eat in the real world. All kinds of parents showed up: married, divorced, foster, adoptive, rich, poor, happy, sad. They were all united in a quest for answers to a riddle that cut like a scalpel across all of their lives: kids. None of those present wanted pie-in-the-sky ideas. They wanted a "just give me the facts, Jack," treatment.

I don't believe they got what they came for. Sure, the ideas were great (!), but I misjudged something about parents that I will never underestimate again. Parents are funny about being told how to do certain things.

You see, I understand parents now. I am one. Parents rear back hissing when you tell them how to raise their kids! I've seen this countless times not only in seminars and in my clinical experience but in the surveys and focus groups I've done for this book. Parents might listen to new and interesting ideas, but if you want to see how long hair gets when it's standing on end, tell them they're doing something wrong with their kids!

This is a peculiar situation. I'm fully aware of your tendency to dismiss what you're told about your boy. There is something very sacred and personal about how we raise our kids, and I'm sensitive to the warning lights flashing on the dashboard of your ego. Unfortunately, too many moms and dads are bellowing about not being told how they will raise little Johnny because too many authorities have challenged their judgment.

I COME IN PEACE! I only want you to win with your boy. And you must understand that the winning path isn't often traveled. I want to offer you an unconventional opportunity to do something remarkable with your son. Consider these ideas "pitches" thrown with the hope that you will swing at them with all your might.

That you've even picked up a book like this suggests three things about you. *First,* you have a boy. You're curious about what this book has to offer and intrigued by the prospect of a unique, helpful, and fresh approach.

Second, you are somewhat of an adventure seeker. You may not look in the mirror and see Indiana Jones, but your desire to aggressively act to improve your boy puts you in an elite league of parents.

Third, you will look for reasons to put this book down. Before I began this book project, I held many meetings with various groups of people to find out what they wanted to know about boys. I got some answers I didn't expect. Perhaps the most pointed reply was, "Just don't waste my time. Tell me anything, especially something fresh, but don't give me a lot of screwy psychology ideas and don't waste my time!"

You are busy trying to raise your boy the best you can, and you haven't got time to drizzle away. If this book doesn't support your need for answers, and do it in a fast and usable way, you will drop it and move on.

Don't put this book down without considering the risks! You hold in your hand the blueprint for creating the next generation of men. It's strictly for changing ordinary boys into extraordinary men—men who can move mountains and, with a focused purpose, change the world.

OUR BOYS ARE IN DEEP PERIL

Our boys are in deep peril. No further evidence need be presented since the events of September 11, 2001. Powerful and hostile forces operate in our world right now. They are bold and stealthy, intent on wrestling greatness from the grasp of our boys. These forces are not always obvious. Collectively, we can learn to spot them and beat them at their game. We can create a generation of boys representing our greatest achievement. As they say, we can hang together, or we can hang alone.

History is filled with examples of victory at hand, only to be lost due to negligence or stubbornness of the leaders. Hitler should have won the war, our federal debt should have been fixed long ago, and the Chicago Cubs should have gone to the World Series by now! Every game, every deal, every interaction, has a critical moment that affects the final outcome. The difference between winning and losing can come down to a small event. Think deeply about yourself.

Don't be a parent who loses the game because he chose to live by ego rather than by possibilities. The stakes are too high. Your boy's life is too valuable to ignore any sensible possibility to make him better.

IT IS EASIER TO RAISE
BOYS THAN TO FIX MEN

I once read that "it is easier to raise boys than to fix men," and I immediately recognized the simple brilliance. Broken men surround us, and they are the focus of intense popular attention. How often have we read about the men's movement, lack of sensitive and informed male leadership in our culture and families, and a general absence of strong male role models in our society? It makes sense to raise boys to be good men, but how, when all we are told we have are discredited examples?

This quotation only hints at the radical nature of the rescue mission that we as parents need to perform. We must swing into action immediately because our boys aren't waiting around for us. They encounter new situations and learning experiences daily that are shaping their collective identity and their individual destiny. We must move to change the course of events now!

For Mom Only

Most child-rearing books are read by women. You could have guessed that, right? Your natural role as a mother puts you in a unique position. You want your son to grow up to be a well-balanced man, but you don't know much about that. You've been a girl your whole life! You are wide open to ideas about how to raise a good boy, and you know that rearing a healthy son requires a team effort where everyone pitches in.

In a perfect "Leave It to Beaver" world, mothers and fathers happily unite in raising their boys and girls. Each partner contributes unique and vital elements. In a perfect world, that is.

In a subperfect world, we are all doing the best we can. That's oftentimes replete with mistakes: fathers who aren't around or who won't stand up and be counted, lousy trade-offs between kids and responsibilities, and a noticeable limp in our walk through child rearing.

I've known many moms raising boys alone. Saying that it's difficult somehow fails to capture all that's involved. I don't know what your particular situation is like. I hope your life is satisfying, but it may be far from it. The good news is, *whether your situation is good or bad doesn't need to have a bearing on how your son eventually turns out.* Plenty of errant boys have sprung from great, unified homes, and many solid young men have come from homes with notoriously poor role models. With that in mind, take some hope that no matter what your circumstance—single, married, divorced, or widowed—you can raise a healthy young man if you know what to do.

Your contribution as a mother involves essentially demonstrating your maternal love for your boy, realizing that what your son sees of you is what he will see of women in general, developing his "softer" side and pushing him toward masculinity. Let's look at each one.

You must actively and freely love your son. It is *the most vital thing* you can do to raise a healthy boy. A boy who knows he is loved can suffer massive tragedy and be all right. But remember this: It doesn't matter how much you say it if he can't hear it. The meaning of "I love you" is how he interprets it. Assume responsibility to make the message clear. Don't allow any ambiguity.

The way your son relates to you creates a beginning point for him to relate to girls in general. You are the ambassador of women to your son. Let him get a balanced view of what womanhood is all about, and let him create a solid relationship with you.

Women are a combination of feminine and masculine traits, and men are a combination of masculine and feminine traits. Each of us to some extent or another shares qualities of the opposite sex.

How does this fact relate to your boy? Help him appreciate what is foreign to him: femaleness. That means intuition, understanding, warmth, emotional depth, perseverance, and courage. This book will help you understand how to build these qualities in the most effective way.

Push your son toward masculinity. You might picture raising a boy as a push-pull arrangement. Due to biological survival, a boy's first attachment is to you, his mother. Dad's role is that of support. As time progresses, Dad (or some other male) takes on a new role of pulling the child toward him. As he pulls (assuming that some male does so), you must push. Give your son permission, encouragement, and support as he makes the vital transition. You know intuitively that you must do this, and this book will show you steps to take.

You are eminently qualified for this job. If you are doing the job all alone, I wholeheartedly welcome you to a great source of insight that will encourage and help you. If you must, you can raise a healthy son alone. Or you may have the help of a man. Your job load will be significantly lighter but no less easy.

Boys need considerable maternal advice and input to be healthy. Forget people who say that boys are mothered too much these days. That happens only in rare cases. It would be more appropriate to say that boys are *underfathered* because that's the glaring problem.

In primitive cultures, when boys become teenagers, they get called out by the elder tribesmen to be trained as men. In civilized cultures, when men become fathers, they need to be called out to join in one of the most amazing rituals life has to offer: raising their sons. You know how important this is. Go to your son's father or another man, and call him out! There's work to be done.

FOR DAD ONLY

I need to talk to you for a moment man-to-man. For most males, such a suggestion conjures an image of trouble. Do yourself a favor and strike that negative image, for what I am about to tell you is the closest you will ever come to giving life.

The whole parenting thing probably came on you by storm. There is no way to adequately prepare for what happens. First there is pregnancy, 99 percent of which leaves you looking at your wife with a mixture of bewilderment and astonishment. Then there is childbirth, the single most unnatural thing a man can ever be involved with!

Then there is the first year; it doesn't seem as though your presence matters to anyone, least of all your baby. It surely seems like an outsider-looking-in deal.

When do you become important? Well, sometime between pushing the stroller and handing over the keys to the car. To be more specific, you are important and valuable as soon as you make yourself important and valuable. Most dads don't discover this until it's too late. It reminds me of a speaker who said there are three kinds of dads: those who make things happen, those who watch things happen, and those who ask what happened!

Most men don't read child-rearing books because these books are way too "soft." Nothing about these fine books appeals to a broad spectrum of men. Think about how many other men you know who have actually sat down and read a child-rearing book. You'll need only one hand to count.

This might be the first and last one you ever read. Let me say that there are things you can do to become the difference between average and awesome for your son. You'll find this book a formula for success—your *son's* success.

Would you like a secret formula that will help you win the biggest race of your life? To raise an exceptional son, you need the right fuel. Of the many ways I could suggest for you to view this book, I'd prefer it to be as a formula for exotic racing fuel. So what is it?

The formula is a series of ingredients that don't come *to* you from this book but that come *from* you. Your boy needs you. He needs your confirmation, your affirmation, and your motivation. Mix well and serve warm. Period. Racing fuel.

Your boy needs your confirmation. That means he is looking to you to tell him that he is all right. Boys, beginning around the age of five, come to men like little sponges. Your boy wants to know that he is worthy, that he is acceptable, that he measures up in your eyes, and that he means something special to you. It takes so little to confirm him. Tell him that he is the greatest, and back it up with your actions.

Your boy needs your affirmation. Remember that he barely knows up from down, and he needs your direction and support to know how to grow. He will beg for such direction in many nonverbal ways, and you must be willing to take a stand and speak into his little life.

Your boy needs your motivation. He needs your brain, your schemes, and your dreams. Give it all to him. If you have no idea how to begin, read on. You have what he wants—you just don't know it yet.

Men and women can benefit from reading this book. But I have gone to great lengths and risked alienating women readers by making this fun and intriguing for men. The future of our world depends on your raising a boy of high caliber. Fix your sights on the real issue: raising a boy fit to change the world.

1 + 1 > 2

In the first grade, the brilliant British mathematical prodigy Bertrand Russell made a spectacle of himself. When the math teacher said, "One plus one equals two," little Berty asked, "Why?" Now, it was not one of those nagging *why* questions that kids routinely ask. He was serious. The teacher could not explain why.

Bertrand Russell went on to write a book called *Principia Mathematica* in which he explained the logic behind one plus one equals two. It was possible, he proved, that one plus one equals two, but more often it was possible that one plus one was *greater* than two! That became the mathematical basis of *synergy*, the modern principle that two or more forces can combine to create a force greater than the sum total of all their energies individually. We need to put that principle in force.

Raising an exceptional boy requires the coordinated action of many people. It's a team effort involving the unity of Mom and Dad and others, including grandparents, teachers, community leaders, and so on. Read this book carefully and coordinate your efforts to make *parental synergy:* action greater than the sum of everyone's efforts.

ACTION TO TAKE Discuss the ideas in this chapter with one other person involved in raising your boy. Talk about your son specifically. Ask for clear, specific input, and by all means take notes on your conversations!

CHAPTER 2

Raising Winners

This chapter zeroes in on the explosive factors related to raising boys. The purpose is to provide background and compelling arguments for performing this mission with delicacy and determination. Raising a boy to be an upstanding man requires thoughtful consideration and wise execution.

WHAT IS A BOY?

We used to have a great family dog named Ashley. She was a high-spirited cocker spaniel mix, and we all loved her deeply. Unfortunately, we had to get rid of her because she picked up a nasty habit: She started biting boys. Not girls, not men or women, not babies, just boys! Why? I hadn't a clue until my older neighbor summarized the situation. "Bill," he said, "I'd bite them, too, if I could catch 'em!"

That experience made me wonder about the essential differences between boys and girls. If I asked you to list the differences between the sexes, I suspect you could compile an extensive and interesting list. If I pressed further and asked you to compile a list of differences between *big boys* and *small boys,* I think the list would be equally extensive. Defining a boy within the context of this book is like staking a claim during gold rush days: You can stake out a definition as large as you like, but you need to be ready to work the entire claim!

We're going to create a reasonably sized, workable claim. Boys are males ages five to twelve. Males younger than five are what I would call babies, and for lots of physical and psychological reasons are so different that we can't easily include them in this discussion. Males older than twelve are teenagers, and their parents know they are entirely different creatures.

Boys are highly explosive. By that, I mean that the average five-to-twelve-year-old boy has potential far beyond what his parents credit him for. He's destined at birth for a spectacular life. He is an intense focus of energy, an adventurer, a laboratory, a sound studio, a puzzle, a playground, a toy, a source of love, and a one-of-a-kind contribution to the world! The boy living in your home is gifted with at least one attribute that sets him apart from all other boys his age. He is easily capable of changing the world and attaining anything in life that he wants.

WHAT'S A GOOD BOY?

All boys are good boys. Now, do me a favor and don't burst out laughing! I say this not from the position of a blind humanitarian but from a position that recognizes the total innocence in which children are brought into this world. They are designable and moldable in an infinite variety of ways. All boys devote much of early life to eagerly collecting information and building basic attitudes and beliefs upon which they will live the rest of life. You play a role in that.

Uncountable numbers of factors and forces intermingle in the minds of boys during these ages. Within this swirling cauldron of experience, boys begin making decisions and living by their abilities. For better or worse, they make the best decisions they can with the information they have available, and they begin the arduous task of learning by experience. They are looking for help, regardless of how independent and carefree they may appear on the outside. Parents and caretakers are in perfect positions to build good boys if they take the time to understand this process and appreciate the forces controlling success.

What's a good boy? Let's not get the water too muddied up here. A good boy is obedient, sensitive, helpful, conversant, polite, and thoughtful—your basic Boy Scout profile. You can depend on him (most of the time) to think clearly, make good decisions, exhibit honesty, and be well rounded and teachable. That is a good boy.

What motivates a young boy to act good? What will make these good attributes viable and survivable throughout his adulthood? How do you teach a boy these traits? The answers to these questions coil and intertwine to form a rope with which your son can lasso excellence.

The large strands in this rope of goodness seem to be

- a personal urge to live up to a high standard
- the developing maturity of the boy
- habits of discipline
- a developed sense of love and caring
- bold, exemplary models

If you read carefully, you will notice that this list is a collection of biologically driven changes and learned behavior. Though I don't think biology and learning are the sum of the developmental forces molding good boys, they provide a clear starting spot from which to begin our discussion.

Good boys acquire sensitivity to the moral value of good behavior. Though it's difficult to pinpoint when and where this hazy and hard-to-define sensitivity is learned, it seems to be a common urge that dominates good boys. It is by no means a constant motivation, but a moral bearing is generally in force in these boys.

The force of maturity is of biological origin. All boys do grow up and, through the seasoning process of life, develop an appreciation of the benefits of good behavior. Most boys learn that those who act in good, acceptable ways get rewarded, and those who don't get penalized. Maturity makes this recognition possible.

All good boys are well disciplined. The root of the word *discipline* is the same root as the word *disciple*. Boys who are disciplined have been taught to be disciples of something or someone. They have been given a clear and unambiguous set of standards to live up to, and they have been shown how to live according to those standards. Disciplined boys are good disciples with good habits. The level of quality to which the disciplined boy develops is proportional to the quality of that to which he is a disciple.

Boys are *not* born to be loving and caring; they are taught. Good boys have been reared to treat others with love and care and act in those ways due to practice.

Good boys typically have bold, exemplary models. From birth until death, we pick and choose aspects of others that we like and admire. The more defined the behaviors of people we admire, the more we are likely to conform to them. This is particularly true about boys, who are constantly on the lookout for new, distinctive, and interesting ways to act. Good boys have had some kind of good behavior modeled by significant individuals in their lives.

WHAT'S A GOOD MAN?

Psychology Today sponsored a fascinating study by Sam Keen and Dr. Ofer Zur in 1989. The study was a poll to discover who were considered ideal men, good men, average men, and inferior men, and what qualities typified each. The results appeared in the November 1989 issue of the magazine and again in Sam Keen's book *Fire in the Belly.* It suggests some interesting opinions.

The top ideal man—by a wide two-to-one margin—was Jesus

Christ. The rest of the list included such people as Gandhi, John F. Kennedy, Thomas Jefferson, Winston Churchill, and Billy Graham. What made them ideal? By a similar two-to-one margin, being caring and loving was first, followed by intelligence, morality/honesty, sensitivity, courage, and a family orientation.

Any surprise? No. Though the institution of manhood has suffered attacks for several decades, consensus on the qualities that make a good man is easy to define. We assign great value to leadership, initiative, courage, good decision making, wisdom and discernment, strength of character, lovingness and kindness, a stance for what one thinks is right, integrity, and provision for the family. These adhesive sorts of traits unite people and societies and press civilized life forward.

A good man is the behavioral enactment of these qualities. Men who are labeled "good" often have an automatic lifestyle of goodness. They don't just "get good" from time to time; they act in good ways on a regular basis. Good men, though not perfect, have habits of goodness and a dependable and active conscience to match. Abe Lincoln summarized his experience with a firm conscience by saying, "When I do good, I feel good. When I don't do good, I don't feel good." Does it get any simpler?

RAISING WINNERS:
HOW DO WE RAISE BOYS INTO GOOD MEN?

What a great question! If the answer to the question were obvious, everyone would recognize it. Raising a winner is not that obvious. It's a fact that winners have been raised out of every conceivable family situation known to humankind. It's a perennial mystery how delightful winners can rise up from ruinous and evil life situations, and losers can plunge down from lives of privilege and success. I am sure that if you want your son to be average, do the average things. If you choose instead for him to be remarkable, your course of action must be equally remarkable.

I suggest eight qualities you must build in now to help your son grow to be a good man and conquer his destiny. That's raising a winner.

Eight Winning Qualities

Eight buildable qualities form the architecture of winning boys:

1. Boys who can relate to their parents

2. Boys who can open up and talk about themselves

3. Boys who can be curious, imaginative, and creative

4. Boys who have disciplined habits

5. Boys who have good attitudes

6. Boys who understand winning and losing through athletics

7. Boys who have complete mastery over one skill

8. Boys who have a spiritual foundation

Boys raised to personify these qualities would be remarkable by any standard, wouldn't you agree? But we can attempt to build a generation of men who are even better than all this. Let's create men who are tough, resourceful, creative, full of drive, and full of care. Hardworking winners they'll be—capable, faithful, and powerful forces in a world working constantly to sidetrack them. Is there a name for men like this? Yes. They are Renaissance men.

WHAT IN THE WORLD IS A RENAISSANCE MAN?

The Renaissance (literally, "rebirth") started in the fourteenth century as the world emerged from the Middle Ages. It was a remarkable moment in history when brave individuals set upon a course to revive traditional elements of goodness and excellence in men. The traditional elements the Renaissance men chose to revive were those that graced ancient Greek and Roman cultures: qualities such as appreciation of and skill in the arts, music, debate, athletic prowess, inventiveness, and creativity. During the Renaissance, the refinement of human ability was the pursuit of the day.

We face a New Renaissance today. It's a fresh and urgent breeze in time that's kicking up. Technological and social changes fly at us in dizzying flocks; the world is shrinking due to communication and population; never-seen-before worldwide economies are forming; the search for meaning and purpose is taunting our sensibilities. What a great time to be alive! What great opportunities exist for men prepared to recognize and master them!

We need Renaissance men to navigate life successfully in the twenty-first century. Answers to the complex and original combination of problems facing us today have yet to be devised. Einstein offered a challenging observation when he said, "The significant problems we face cannot be solved with the same level of thinking we were at when we created them." If there was ever a time that the world needed a new breed to step forward and assume leadership, it is now. The world is moving forward forcefully, and only forceful men will be able to lay a hand on it. Make your boy one of them! Let the excitement begin!

SET YOUR SIGHTS ON THE FUTURE . . .

In my years of counseling, I learned two simple equivalents: (1) The past equals boredom, and (2) the future equals hope and excitement.

"Water over the dam" has a distinctive air of stagnation. You can do nothing about it except analyze it for mistakes or dream about what could have been. Doesn't that sound depressing? The future is another matter. It seems a general human trait to get interested in and excited about what could happen in the future. Maybe it's for hope, the chance to make good on wishes and dreams hidden deep within a frail human heart. All I know is that when you mention the future and doing something good with it, even eyes suffering from years of oppression and pain begin again to sparkle.

My obsession is with tomorrow. *Boys!* aims at tomorrow and takes us sprinting directly into the future. You must learn to feel that acceleration and not look back. I've worked professionally with race car drivers, and I met one with a peculiar attitude about rearview mirrors. He didn't like to have them on the car, let alone use them, because in his words, "What's behind me doesn't matter!"

My intention is for you to stop treating your brain as a rearview mirror and start using it as a lightning generator. The action is in front of you, and that is the proper place to apply your energies.

. . . AND RUN AS HARD AS YOU CAN!

There's a saying: "If you're not the lead dog, the scenery never changes." The sad truth about the job we have before us is that the world doesn't really care about you or your boys. The world doesn't care if you're a leader or a follower, a success or a flop, or anything else. The world needs to force you into a rut because, from its perspective, that's the safest place for you. If you're out of sight, you can't cause any trouble!

A principle in cybernetics (communications theory) is called *requisite variety.* Requisite variety states that the element or variable with the greatest degree of flexibility in a system will control the whole system. For instance, if you consider all the parts of the radio, the piece with the greatest degree of flexibility is probably the volume knob. Of all the pieces of a radio, guess which piece has the greatest control? With computers, it's probably the keyboard. In societies of people, it's the person with the greatest degree of personal initiative.

You are not a robot born into this world to react thoughtlessly. You are a unique human being with one quality that is your greatest asset: the initiative to choose. You are the point man, the team leader, the coach, the captain who is making choices and calling the shots. You capitalize on requisite variety every time you pull the trigger and choose to act. Understand that the people around you (including your boy) are probably waiting to be told what to do. They need to be led, and they are waiting for the person with a purpose to step forward and pull the trigger.

I believe your choice boils down to an issue of love. Do you love your boy enough to stretch above and beyond the call of duty and attempt something great?

ACTION TO TAKE

You must consciously make a new choice to help your son sail in the seas of the New Renaissance. Sit down with him and tell him what you are going to do and why. Tell him that you two are going to take an adventure together that will last a lifetime.

CHAPTER 3

An Unconventional Approach

More enslaved than the Hebrews, more oppressed than the Persians, more scattered than the Athenians; without head, without order, beaten, despoiled, pillaged, and torn, and overrun by foreign powers . . . The situation is critical, but the opportunity is ripe. [The people] are willing to follow a banner if only someone will raise it!

—Machiavelli, The Prince

We have not men fit for the times. We are deficient in Genius, in Education, in Gravity, in Fortune, in Everything. I feel unutterable anxiety. God grant us wisdom and fortitude.

—John Adams, prior to the American Revolution, 1774

Let your eyes look straight ahead,
And your eyelids look right before you.
Ponder the path of your feet,
And let all your ways be established.

—Proverbs 4:25–26

Mistakes are made in parenting, but solutions are available. The unconventional path will be a stretch for you, but raising a winner is clearly within your grasp.

FIVE CLASSIC PARENTING BOO-BOOS

Getting your boy from point A to point Z on the Renaissance road demands that you first figure out where you are. I want to discuss five general patterns of parenting that represent where most parents find themselves. These aren't particularly good patterns, but if you find yourself here, don't dissolve in worry; it may actually be good news! At least you can know where you are presently located and that the cavalry is coming! Just keep remembering that few things are permanent, least of all a parenting problem. I'll outline the foul patterns now and offer corrections shortly.

Boo-Boo #1: All Talk / No Action

You'll pay a very high price for doing nothing for your boy. I'm always flabbergasted at the number of parents I see practicing laissez-faire parenting. They evidently have no understanding of the risks they are exposed to. If you don't mind having life steamroll your boy, I suppose talking big and doing nothing for him are acceptable.

Unfortunately, to remain comfortable with ourselves, we say that we are doing the best that we can do. We become experts not in taking action but in persuading ourselves that under the circumstances, we are giving our best effort. This is usually a flawless self-con job. It chokes off parental effectiveness by allowing us to think we're contributing to the lives of our kids when we're not. The only antidote is radical self-honesty.

How do you know if you are a well-meaning but do-nothing parent? If you have the greatest intentions in the world, but your boy is still going nowhere. Your intentions are only as good as the outcomes they generate. If your boy is not visibly improving or moving in a positive direction, you are doing nothing. Be honest with yourself.

Boo-Boo #2: No Vision / No Plan

The story is told of a group of dignitaries visiting the newly opened Disney World in Orlando, Florida, sometime after the death of Walt Disney. Walt Disney's son was conducting the tour, during which a member of the entourage commented how sad it was that Walt had died without seeing the finished attraction. Walt Disney's son stopped a moment to think, then replied, "He did see it when it was completed; that's why it's here."

Too many of us live completely by accident rather than by a goal. "Life by default," I call it. That's when life just happens to you: no plan, no system, no vision. Letting the forces of life force your life. People stuck in this trap are ones we all fear to be: the infamous "quietly desperate."

If you don't decide what your visions and plans for your son will be, someone else will decide for you. Your best intentions are not necessarily what the world values, and your son is not on the world's list of top priorities.

Boo-Boo #3: Bolts-in-the-Neck Parenthood

We are all familiar with the classic tale of Frankenstein's monster. He was that pieced-together guy with a hot temper and a bad tailor. He was more or less the creation of a brilliant scientist who thought that he could create life by an odd combination of surgery and lightning. Does this relate to parenting?

Many of our parenting plans are as pieced together as Frankenstein's monster. We take a little time here, a little effort there, and we sew it together and call it parenthood. Get the picture? The only things missing are the bolts in the neck!

If your parenting fits together like the monster, don't be surprised if your son runs away screaming.

Boo-Boo #4: The Lights Are On and No One's Home

Dr. Benjamin Spock observed, "Members of this society place too much confidence in the child-rearing establishment." Child-rearing psychology in America is a large, profitable industry. It offers us many products in the form of educational helps, video training, therapies, and more. Part of the "sell" of these products is to convince the public that what it is doing is wrong and that the new way is a better way. And historically, the public has swallowed the line.

Thoughtlessness among parents usually takes the form of fuzzy-mindedness. We often lack clear, thoughtful rationale for the actions we undertake. It can be as simple as neglecting to think about the impact of our beliefs and actions to willfully abandoning critical thought altogether. We often choose to judge correctness of new parenting ideas according to the prevailing fad. This herd mentality is responsible for substantial family chaos.

Boo-Boo #5: Letting Time Steal Your Life

The mismanagement of time steals your life in sneaky ways. Time is an experienced flier: Your son grows up too fast, there are never moments to do what you want to do, and before you stop to notice, life has glided quietly out the back door.

It robs first by orienting your obsessions with the "here and now," to the detriment of the future. The present moment has a compelling, almost gravitational pull on your attention. You never seem to escape it long enough to plan for tomorrow, let alone a legacy for the generations to follow.

And what does time do to your beliefs? What might you believe to be true ten years from now? Will it be what you believe today? Life seems to creep and change with imperceptible slowness. You shed layer after layer of beliefs like a snake sheds skin, all without even a blink of awareness. This is the chief operating mode of the thief of time.

Here is yet a third angle: The next ten, twenty, thirty years will bring changes you cannot begin to predict. Your values, beliefs, and biases will all undergo sharp changes due to unforeseeable life experiences: compromised commitments, quivering aims, and drifting goals. Not because you are a bad person, mind you, but because time is sweeping past and you haven't the means to harness it. This is a problem requiring a swift response. Stop the thief *now*. Your son won't be a boy long.

THE UNCONVENTIONAL PATH

A group was going on a backcountry wilderness exploration in Canada. The people arrived at the outfitter's camp on the edge of the woods and spent the morning preparing packs and supplies for the long trek. But there was a problem. A member of the expedition noticed that the guide lacked maps for the backcountry they would explore.

No maps! To make matters worse, no compass! They anxiously approached the guide with their growing worry, but he looked confidently at them and smiled. "Maps and compasses are not the way through these mountains," he announced. "I am the way through the mountains."

The unconventional path to raising a boy into a good man is you! You're tailored to your task, raised to it, and bred with the ideals for it since childhood, though you don't know it yet. But you do recognize distinction when you see it. You recognize excellence when it's in front of you. You can spot the above average quickly. That, my friend, is the beginning of raising a Renaissance man.

I offer five unconventional replies to the boo-boos of parenthood. They will keep you on the unconventional path.

1. You Need to Keep the Unconventional Path Simple

We have a tendency to grant higher status and respect to complex answers than to simple ones. We seem to assume that the more complex an answer appears, the more correct it must be. To confine the folly of this human weakness, a brilliant medieval monk named William of Ockham proposed what is now called Ockham's razor. Properly stated, it says, "A plurality is not to be posited without necessity." Translated, that means that when we're given a choice between two competing correct answers to a problem, the more correct is the simpler of the two.

Diagnosing what children might need to grow is fairly easy, and deciding on a course of action is simple. The treatment takes talent and intuition. If we follow the dictates of Ockham's razor, the better path of growth is the simple path.

Interacting with your son involves an astronomical number of choices. Should you play it safe or do something radical? Risk going all out or be conservative to avoid possible error and trouble? These and other questions must be answered. What's the correct option to choose? That's unanswerable. This much you can be sure of, however: The more choices of which you avail yourself, the better are your chances of selecting a successful course. Fear of change is the most prominent cause for lack of options from which to choose.

We're notoriously allergic to the fear inherent in change. As a consequence, we don't create new choices for ourselves, and we don't experiment with the vast horizons of possibilities to influence our kids. Instead we apply two or three pat and safe ways of interaction, never really sensing all the other choices we have before us. I want to illuminate some of the new choices and create in you the courage to attempt to do things you've never dreamed possible.

2. You Can Stretch Farther Than You Think

In my home, I don't measure the kids' height from where they stand to the top of the head; I measure from where they stand to where they reach! You've never seen kids stretch so far! Do me a favor. Go to a nearby wall, and with a pencil reach up as high as you can and mark the wall where you peak. Do it now.

Now, go back and stretch yourself another one-half inch. You can do it! You could move yourself up two inches if you used some creativity.

This is a bedrock of wisdom upon which you will build a parental dynasty. You can stretch the performance of any of your senses or abilities, just as you physically stretch your body. You can stretch your imagination, your drive, your stubbornness, your love, and your patience. Stretching yourself is a core element in delivering your best effort to your son. Your best is how far you stretch.

You can always do more than you think. Can you do *anything?* Of course not. You're a real-world person, and you know that your stretching does have limits. All you can do is all you can do. But you can push yourself sensibly, stretching in areas that have a high probability of noticeable impact. Stretch yourself wisely, and do a few things exceptionally well.

3. A Boy Needs a Coach, Mentor, and Hero

When a boy is born, he needs nurturing, motherly care that the father cannot offer. Dad's role is limited at the start, except to play a support role for the mother and what she is doing. Dad's importance, however, grows exponentially after the first years of life.

As a boy grows through the first five years of life, the scene begins to change. He begins to have needs for what Dad offers that Mother can't fulfill. A boy in this period doesn't need a mothering daddy. He needs a man who is decisive, fun, and willing to stand up and be counted. He needs a coach, mentor, and hero.

A coach teaches, inspires, cajoles, demands, encourages, pushes, and leads. Good coaches can create great performances in ordinary people. We build statues to and heap great honor on those who have the patience and strength to mold men and women into champions.

It's a great virtue to create (coach) people who in sports or life "play over their heads," "reach for the stars," and are willing to work for their dreams.

A mentor is a tutor and a model—somebody with a special interest in the boy, a skill to teach, and a willingness to do so. Most boys will seek out adult men to fulfill master-apprentice relationships in their lives. You can fill that role if you choose to be available to your son.

What about a hero? Do you remember those old war movies where a group of soldiers are squatting in a foxhole and in comes a live grenade? All eyes bulge in fear as a mad scramble erupts. Just before detonation, one brave soul selflessly dives on the thing, losing his life and making himself an instant legend. The stories of these exploits (many of them true) are riveting. Why? These men are heroes. They don't have grand ideologies or complex motives. We lionize their demonstrations of courage and immortal action, but they don't see themselves as special. They see a job and do it. They care deeply, a sure anesthetic for the pain they often endure. They're perfectly willing to sacrifice themselves for those they care about.

You're probably the only hero your boy will ever personally know. You love your boy intensely, and you are more than likely willing to sacrifice your life for his. His life, after all, is more important than yours.

God has designed us to need something worth dying for. It is the root motivation for heroism. Your son didn't choose you, and you didn't choose him. But you're together for life, and nothing can change that. He needs someone to be his hero because the world is beginning to rain grenades on him. Make your move.

4. Your Attitude Is the Defining Factor

Though this idea might not sound stirring or unconventional on the surface, consider this exemplary and wise story:

Once a farmer was out working in his fields when along down the road came a tired-looking man.

"Where ya goin', stranger?" the farmer asked.

The man leaped back, startled, and with a trembling voice and bulging eyes replied, "T-T-To the next town. What are people like in the next town?"

"What were they like in the last town?" the farmer asked.

"They were all mean and cruel, and I didn't like them at all," the stranger blurted.

The farmer sadly shook his head and looked down. "I'm afraid you'll find the people of the next town to be the same way."

A few days later, another man came down the same road. "How ya doin', stranger?" the farmer asked, to which the stranger replied, "Very good, sir. Thank you for asking. Say, what do you know of the people in the next town?"

The farmer looked at him for a moment and asked wisely, "What were they like in the last town you were in?"

"Oh, my! They were very friendly and kind to me, and I enjoyed them very much!" replied the stranger.

A smile came to the farmer's face, and he said, "You'll find the people of the next town to be exactly the same way."

Do you get the message? "Say there, stranger, what kind of kid do you have, and where is he going?"

5. It Doesn't Pay to Quit

Don't ever forget that the world *wants* you to quit. It's the only safe place for you. Don't quit. Golda Meir, former prime minister of Israel, said of the utter fierceness of the Israeli military, "We have a secret weapon in our struggle . . . We have no place to go."

The unconventional Renaissance plan will challenge your innovation and patience daily. You need to use all your bravery and wisdom and faith to succeed. You can't be a second-string parent and expect this plan to work.

I have days when I feel terribly lazy, I get mad, I get distracted and irritable, I get in ruts, and I'm proven wrong. Confusion and intimidation are my frequent colleagues. But I don't quit. I can't. Neither should you, even in your darkest moments. If you have one motto from which you never sway, it should be this: "It doesn't pay to quit."

Dag Hammarskjöld said, "Life demands from you only the strength you posess. Only one feat is possible—not to have run away."

ACTION TO TAKE

Take the unconventional path. Do you have anything special to offer your son? If your answer is "no" or "I'm not sure," you'd better reread this chapter. You have plenty to offer, but you may have never been told how.

CHAPTER 4

What Keeps Boys from Succeeding?

The worst way to fail on the Renaissance journey is to be stopped. If you want to win, find out how your problems operate and set about preparing for them. If you know what's coming and prepare, you and your son cannot be stopped.

MAXIMUM MANHOOD IS NORMAL

A few years ago, my family and I were eating breakfast at a local diner. The regulars were perched at the counter drinking coffee and smoking stale cigarettes. We took our seats in a booth, and right in my line of sight was a dilapidated older fellow with unkempt clothes, an overgrown beard, and a distant gaze in his eyes. How appetizing.

My son Jake was opposite me on the other side of the booth, and he kept getting a strange smile streaking across his face. Then he'd turn red and duck his head. Jake kept up the routine throughout the whole meal, so I finally asked him to let me in on the gag.

He turned red and ducked his head. I gave him my "what's the matter with you?" look, and he replied with that Cheshire cat smile all the boys have. Kathi leaned over toward me and told me to look behind me. I slowly turned around, and to my surprise, I saw a very cute ten-year-old girl turning red and ducking her head!

It dawned on me that we all came to the same restaurant together, all sat together, all ate together, but all had completely different views of the affair. Jake's view was of a cute girl set against the background of bright windows, flowers, and gently blowing trees in the distance. Me? I was looking back into a dark corner at a guy struggling his way through a messy breakfast. I should have changed seats and gotten a new perspective.

Healthy manhood is a normal thing to grow toward, so asking how to get there is a strange question. A more sensible perspective would be to analyze the detours that could tempt a boy on his journey to manhood. This is such a refreshing perspective. What will stop your son from naturally gaining his full potential as a man? What styles or habits should be avoided to stay on the natural road to manhood? What about you, the cheerleader along the Renaissance road? How might you unintentionally hinder his success? These are wonderful questions that make sense only within a common understanding about what constitutes victory.

How Shall We Think of Success?

Understanding victory starts with a conversation about competition. The world organizes itself by the outcomes of countless competitions. There are generally two forms of competitions. First are competitions against yourself, and second are competitions against others. Competitions against yourself are challenges like getting out of bed in the morning, losing weight, and remembering to pick up the kids by five o'clock. Competitions against other people are activities like getting a good parking spot, persuading people to see things your way, and fighting for some time alone.

If you stop and think, you invest your time every day in some form of competitive exercise. Most of these competitions serve the general purpose of living life.

Now enter winning. The world is like a ruthless fight promoter. It doesn't care if you win or lose; it just wants to see a good fight! The world is responsible for defining that *winning is how well you compare to someone else.* Winning means having competitions conclude in your favor. For better or worse, you learn to focus on others and your relative positions to them.

However, true victory and success ultimately need to be assessments you make about yourself, internally and emotionally, without anyone else present. In the final analysis, the judgment of how successful you have been rests on whether you have lived up to what you believe to be your capabilities.

The ultimate decision about whether your life is a success will come when you compare your life against your talents and potentials. It won't come by highlighting your successes, it won't come by counting the number of cars in your garage or measuring the square footage of your house, and it won't come by focusing solely on your mistakes and faults. It will be just you and the person in the mirror, and at that instant you are going to make a judgment about what you could have been despite the obstacles.

What will be your response when you ask: Did I give life my best effort? To say yes will produce a sense of gratification reserved for your wildest dreams. To say no condemns you to a life of second-guessing. Perhaps you are familiar with some research that was done on retired persons in a nursing home with respect to what they regretted most in life. The most commonly reported regret by a large margin was "not taking enough chances in life." Translation: "I wish I had done more with what I had."

Your son wants to be like successful people he knows. Inside his heart kindle dreams and desires you know nothing about. I played a pickup baseball game with some neighborhood kids not too long ago, and one boy kept saying he wanted to be "Jim." I thought maybe he knew my father-in-law. I had never seen him throw the ball before, and he was terrible! He threw left-handed, holding his mitt in his right armpit. After he threw the ball, he quickly switched his mitt onto his left hand and played the hit. "What are you doin', buddy?" I asked. "This is the way Jim Abbott does it," he said. (Jim Abbott is the left-handed major-league pitcher who lacks a right hand.) I thought he threw the ball as he did because his dad never played with him!

Boys naturally model themselves after people they see doing what they aspire to. Unless taught otherwise, they will judge their success based on the world's external standards of relative position. That will never give them the sense of achievement and success they strive for.

How Big Can He Dream?

To teach your son to compete against himself, you start by determining what he thinks he's capable of, how far he has come along that road, and what is going to stop him from getting where he wants to go. Determine these and you will have helped him create a very effective means of applying his energies.

We all have ideas of what we want to do in our lives, and chances are good that your son has some wild plans. At this point in his life, the wilder, the better. Encourage him to think big. Don't tell him what to think; just make whatever it is BIG! Avoid squashing the ridiculous-sounding things he might dream up. The world has plenty of cold water to throw on his plans without you adding yours. Besides, he might surprise you. Your job at this point is to coach him through the first stage of getting out of life what he wants.

What's going to keep him from achieving his dreams? Plenty.

You and Your Son Are on a Renaissance Road Littered with Mines

What will keep your son from getting where he wants to go? If you effectively anticipate this answer, you and he cannot be stopped! You can prepare and plan around all the defeating influences. If you don't anticipate the answer, *BOOOMMM!*

If you think you can effectively negotiate this trick road alone, bon voyage! I salute your courage. But I don't want to find a bomb crater in the road with two pairs of smoking boots sitting on the edge! Be a little wary; it's smart. Let's take a closer look.

Assume that there is an upper limit to what you as a parent can do for your boy. That means there is a point where you have done all you can humanly do to help your son. You can do no more after that point except cut him loose and pray. When does that cut-loose time arrive? All too soon.

You have your son only a few years of his life, and your impact is physically limited. You must try to reach the upper limits of what you can do as quickly as possible.

Knowing specifically what will stop each movement provides a locations map of the land mines that can blow you both off the road. Having this map can be a source of great confidence and boldness on the road to victory. Let's look at some forces that will keep your son from success.

Having No Plan

I have already spoken to some extent about how having no plan affects parenting. As for your son, the most troubling aspect involves two problems. First, without a clear plan he has no idea what he's trying to accomplish; therefore, he has no way of measuring whether he's succeeded. Boys need to be told it's time to accomplish specific goals. They don't think much about tomorrow. They must be trained how to set up a goal, how to reach it, and how to evaluate progress. A simple written plan serves this objective well.

Second, if he doesn't have a direction or plan, he can't respond to roadblocks and troubles. If your boy doesn't know what he's trying to accomplish with his efforts, the troubles in his life make no sense. Normal everyday challenges will make him feel picked on or victimized if he has no plan. Normal everyday challenges suddenly make lots of sense when he sees that they are stopping him from getting something specific in his life. That kind of problem is much easier to respond to than one that comes out of the blue.

By the way, I don't see any purpose in making your son into a goal-driven, type-A roboboy. That's not what boyhood is about. But being totally without any organized thought about tomorrow is equally unfair.

A mission sentence allows you to dance on the fine line between the two extremes. A mission sentence summarizes what your son wants to do with his tomorrows. It focuses him and grounds him. It should be clear enough to suggest a course of action and provide a means of verifying his achievement.

The secret is to make your son create an absurdly simple sentence and post it someplace. "I want to have fun today," written in dry-erase marker on the bathroom mirror, will do nicely. (It comes off easily.) The point is not so much to create a grand plan for life (he's a boy, remember) but to introduce him to the idea of a plan. It should be specific enough to provide ideas about what he might want to achieve but broad enough to allow for changes. Try things like, "I want to beat Billbo next door in a race," or "I want to save ten dollars for new skates," and so on.

Let your son create his own sentences. Encourage him to have as many as he likes. A mission sentence creates standards to reach for.

Then, ask your boy about the headway he's making on his missions. Remind him of what he stated he wanted to do, and ask if there is anything you can do to help. Asking him to measure his progress on a personal mission sentence is imperative. How else can your son know if he needs to be working differently to reach his goal?

Ignoring the Analysis of Outcomes

I heard a story of a scientist at Harvard who was trying to find the difference between rats and boys. He created an experiment in which the rats got cheese by pressing a steel bar and boys got dollar bills for doing the same action. At one point, the scientist stopped giving rewards for pressing the bar, and the rats quickly stopped pressing the bar. They quietly collected their books and left the laboratory. The boys are still in the laboratory pressing the bar!

I want to suggest a rule that you teach your son immediately. If what you are doing is not working, do something different! This idea might sound idiotically simple. It is. Perhaps that's the reason so many boys (and adults) miss it. If boys think some procedure or idea is supposed to work a certain way, they (like us) will blindly believe it without checking whether it actually works in practice or not.

This is particularly true in attaining goals or solving problems. Teach your son to understand that even advice you think is fail-safe will fail from time to time. I guarantee that everything that works like a charm for you will not always have the same effect for your son. He needs to have the patience to try different avenues if what is supposed to work is failing. Inform him that he has permission to be as creative as necessary to succeed.

Being Inflexible in His Personal Behavior

Along similar lines as not noticing outcomes is stubbornly retaining inflexibility in behavior. People changers will tell you that the major hurdle in helping others grow is developing new behaviors, new ways of thinking and acting. People get clichéd in their behavior and won't try anything new. Boys in particular gravitate into grooves or patterns of behaving and don't try new things, which leads to stagnation and atrophy in their lives.

Let me give you an illustration. I worked with one boy who was a chronic grump. He had the same boring routine each day, which he performed with little deviation or thought. It was no surprise to me that he was such a grouch; I would be, too, if my life were so predictable and plain. I suggested that he try something: walk home from school by a new route. No big deal, right? It was to him! The thought of breaking out of the rut was fearful, confusing, and too energy consuming.

It took me three weeks to convince him, but he finally tried it. It was a glorious day of freedom for the kid, for he allowed himself the chance to find out how being flexible opened up worlds of new opportunity and interest. He found an ice-cream store on the way home that he never knew existed.

To help your son understand flexibility and avoid a land mine, teach him about chains in life. You know what chains are, though the usage might be a little novel. One time I made two pizzas for my kids. I made them exactly the same way except I varied one element in the chain. Using crust, sauce, and cheese, I made the first pizza, and it was cooked twenty minutes at 325 degrees. The second pizza was made with crust, sauce, and cheese, and it was cooked thirty-five minutes at 325 degrees. Changing one part in the chain of events of pizza making made the end products quite different.

Our lives are like pizza recipes. If any event is to proceed in a certain way, a certain chain of action must be exactly followed. Change the order of the chain in the slightest way, and the whole outcome changes. If there is anything about your son's life that causes dissatisfaction and he wants to change, he needs to be flexible enough to change one aspect of his behavior, and the whole pizza of life changes taste!

Having Small Dreams

Dreaming for the future is something that normally evaporates with advancing manhood. That happens when boyhood dreams get stomped on without an adult to offer encouragement. At the core of this trouncing is the reality that it's easier to dream things up than to have them. Sure, most eight-year-olds want to play in the major leagues, but the reality of getting there is different from the dreaming. We've all gone through it, and for that reason we all feel the pain our boys experience when their cherished hopes are dashed away.

To protect your boy from excessive pain, you may encourage him to dream realistically. If you do this with your son, you carelessly stomp out one of God's greatest fires. In a thousand realistic ways, you may crush imagination and big dreams, and make your boy read off your agenda in life. While your son is still young and pliable, light his fuse and get out of the way!

Let his mind soar and fly to places beyond your imagination. Encourage him to forget being realistic. Encourage him to dream BIG!

Keeping Bad Company

Many great boys are blown to smithereens on this mine. Bad company corrupts good character.

My son was hanging around with some bad characters one time, so I told him a story you should remember. I told him about a guy who was hiking up a mountain when a snake came out of the weeds. The snake asked if he could have a ride to the top of the mountain because his stomach was sore. The man was smart and said, "No, you're a snake, and you'll bite me." The snake calmly assured the hiker that he would not bite him if he would just give him a ride. The hiker finally agreed, and up they went.

When they got to the top of the mountain, the hiker bent to put the snake down, and the snake reared back and bit him on the hand! The hiker leaped back with shock and fell to the ground, dying of the venom. With bulging disbelief in his eyes and fear in his voice, he screamed, "Why did you bite me? You promised you wouldn't bite me, and now I'm going to die!"

The snake curled his evil lips and hissed, "You knew I was a snake when you picked me up. Snakes lie and snakes bite."

Don't expect your son to readily accept your diagnosis of his pals. My kids are free to choose their friends. They are not free from my opinion and input. Thank goodness, boys don't want trouble; they want fun and friends. Bad company usually shows its stripes quickly, making it possible to teach about friendship at clear and opportune moments. If a particular friend is being a jerk, remind your son of the snake.

If You Could Teach Him Only One Thing

If you could teach your son only one thing in his life, teach self-discipline. Let's define it as making himself do things he would rather not do. Self-discipline is like an artery running through every aspect of his life, feeding and nourishing what it can reach. Like a developing circulatory system in a new baby, self-discipline should be a part of all that your boy does. It's an unseen source of life.

Let's extend this metaphor. Lack of self-discipline is a common feature of all boys. The extent of that lack of discipline might surprise you. If left completely on his own, a boy won't do much more than make himself comfortable. Just like in arterial growth, something must force the advancement of self-discipline into every area of his life including work, studying, friendship, honesty, commitment, chivalry, and others. The force must be you.

ACTION TO TAKE

The list of things that will stop your boy is fairly short. Make it your business to memorize the list of roadblocks in this chapter. There will be moments in the future when it will call out to you and provide some helpful answers.

CHAPTER 5

What Keeps Parents from Succeeding?

Raising winners is like running for touchdowns in a football game. It's acceptable to get tackled when you can see what's happening, but it's aggravating to get blindsided one yard from the goal line. You don't want to look back on this part of your life and say, "If only I had known." This will help you see what you may not know is about to tackle you.

TRICKLE-DOWN PARENTS

It should be no great revelation that what affects you, good or bad, has a trickle-down effect on your boy. Separating your lives is impossible. For that reason I've included this short discussion to highlight factors that will keep you from reaching the upper limits of influence with your boy.

GET CRITICAL

Honest ignorance of helpful knowledge is the major obstacle to your doing all you can do. We all possess reasonable intelligence, agreed? If there is an overarching architecture of failure in raising winners, it's ignoring information that is useful in making intelligent and powerful choices. Having complete information provides the first major opportunity in reaching the upper limits of positive influence.

People have an irritating tendency when it comes to learning, though. They tend to read lists, remember the high points, and forget the rest. They don't critically evaluate information, they're lackluster in applying intelligent appraisal, and they don't immediately work the information into specific applications. This is a brilliant formula for forgetfulness.

The following information is most useful and powerful if read critically. Think through these ideas, evaluate the logic, challenge the thinking if necessary, think of examples of applications in your home, and consider the implications. It's better for you to reject something on this list because you think it's senseless than to do it because I say so.

This section suggests what will impede you in successfully coaching your son through the Renaissance journey. Memorizing this list won't deposit the information in the part of your brain that needs it. Critical thinking will.

Unawareness of Natural Biological Developments

Guiding your boy requires sensitivity about what changes naturally in him over time and how the changes progress. The biologically driven developments go on in full view, but you may have little recognition and less control.

I've often consulted with parents who were horrified over a perfectly normal change they saw in their child. A few years ago when I was doing some counseling work, I had a rash of kids talking to themselves. Oh, no! Somebody must have written a book about it because many parents were really concerned. I'll never forget one father telling me that he overheard his son saying, "Rumba, rumba, rumba," a lot. *Hmmm, that's really weird,* I thought.

I brought the kid into my office and asked him about the "rumba" stuff. He said he was doing it because it made his mouth feel funny. *Oh, what a hoot!* I screamed to myself. If only his mom and dad could hear that! "This week I want you to try something else that feels good to your mouth. Repeat, 'Bossa nova, bossa nova, bossa nova.'" He said okay and left my office.

Three days later, the frantic dad called me on the phone and said, "Guess what he's saying now!"

You need a quick overview of child development. Not a college version, but an in-the-trenches version. Understanding biological changes happening with your boy provides knowledge in what you can and cannot control. You can then cleanly hurdle another mine on the road to building a great boy. When an age-specific observation is in order, I'll mention it. If some aspect of thinking or behaving shifts or changes with age, I'll mention that as well.

Please take note: After observing thousands of children and parents, I've concluded that "chips off the old block" are rare. You could be the most sedate and controlled individual in the world and have a spontaneity-loving son. "He's like his great-grandfather," you curtly assure yourself. On the other hand are kids who are quiet and frail born to loud, burly, and quarrelsome parents. Don't be too concerned if your son is a lot like you or very different from you. If there is a similarity, it's only an illusion! You are who you are; and he is who he is.

A Combat Prep Look at Child Development. All the general developments I'm going to discuss will go on with or without you. I have discovered that parents are most frightened by the normal and natural consequences of development they don't know about. These changes are to a large extent biologically governed and subject to little outward manipulation. I think this is God's way of ensuring that we can't mess up our kids!

The Development of a Boy's Thinking. You need an understanding of the development of logic and general intelligence. But be forewarned.

I am going to be zipping through a topic that occupies volumes of scientific theory and fact. You are getting the boiled-down treatment necessary to operate effectively.

Natural biological development constrains boys to progress erratically from infantile thinking to adult-style thinking over the five- to twelve-year range. They start this phase of life thinking in a very concrete, here-and-now sensory-based style. This is very different from how you and I think as adults. As maturity proceeds in fits and starts, boys improve at abstract thinking (thinking in the absence of sensory input), finally going over a hump between eight and eleven years old. Higher forms of adult-style logic then become possible. Just remember that mature minds result from growth in a slow, stuttered fashion.

Around the third and fourth grades, boys go through a trying transition. Good sense and good judgment are qualities we expect in an adult frame of thinking. Don't expect these automatically from your son, for he is unable to consistently or effectively think in these ways.

Boys can only solve problems that they can get their hands on. They have a hard time with common sense, abstract reasoning, thinking ahead, and so on until the tail end of the boy's phase of life. These are qualities way beyond what boys can grasp right now, tangibly in front of them.

A few years ago we were at the beach. At the end of the day, my younger son, Zac, dried off and prepared to go home, except that he had sand all over his feet. I told him that he would have to clean off his feet before he put on his shoes. Very obediently, he took his shoes down to the lake, waded in up to his knees, and sat down to wash off his toes. After a minute or two of scrubbing, he put his shoes on, stood up, and came sloshing out of the water. When he got to me, he was soaking wet, and his feet were covered with sand again! When you speak, kids hear what they can hear and make sense in ways that might be completely without adult logic.

General intelligence is a different story. It too has a developmental pattern, and it too relates to the development of abstract reasoning ability. But I need to introduce a significant twist. Many parents get concerned about their boy's intelligence quotient (IQ), and there are many misunderstandings that deserve clarification.

The IQ is a measure representing a ratio of chronological age and mental ability. In the collective public mind, IQ indicates how smart your kid is. It's our means for comparing one another. In the last few years, a controversy has developed about what the scores really indicate. Critics believe (and there are many critics!) that the accepted tests of IQ measure only certain kinds of intelligence. The critics challenge the general validity of the tests, claiming that they test only verbal and mathematical intelligences. The more skilled a child is with the language and logic, the better the child will perform on the test. Therefore, they say IQ is not a fair or an accurate measurement of general intelligence.

The implication here is that there are many kinds of intelligences, and it might be unfair to assert that verbal intelligence is the best or most practical form in which to measure general intelligence.

Howard Gardner, a well-respected and prolific Harvard psychologist, presents some radical ideas in his book *Frames of Mind*. He suggests an appealing alternative to this crude means of classifying intelligence. In his book he suggests that there are at least six intelligences with which to measure people! Everybody has all of them to a greater or lesser extent. That means that everybody is good at some of them and not so good at others.

Linguistic intelligence involves your ability to use and understand the native language, which includes speech, comprehension of nuances, innuendo, synonyms, and creativity with words. Perhaps you know of people gifted in this intelligence, such as speakers, writers, storytellers, and salespeople.

Musical intelligence represents a special form of intelligence with respect to sound. Musical intelligence is having good pitch perception, a sense of rhythm and tempo, and accurate recognition and production of timbre (specific qualities of a tone).

Logical-mathematical intelligence is having skill with numbers, manipulating sets of figures and pieces by a pattern of rules, and applying symbolic reasoning. Einstein was considered a rather dull student because he didn't begin to speak till very late in childhood. (I remind my kids of this!) But his logical-mathematical brilliance allowed him to make wonderful contributions in his field.

Spatial intelligence reflects a great command of many dimensions of space. Persons with spatial intelligence have a good sense of depth, can imagine things in many (more than three) dimensions, and generally have a great degree of sensitivity about what is around them. This may not sound like an intelligence alone, but consider the difficulty you might have with ordinary life without the ability to think and problem-solve in three dimensions, or perceive and understand the relationship between objects in your environment.

Bodily-kinesthetic intelligence is sports aptitude and physical ability. This sort of intelligence represents the ability to move the body through space, and sense and feel the interactions between body and environment. Athletes are therefore brilliant. Dancers and performers are, too. These people express superiority in an unusual area of intelligence.

The *personal intelligences* could easily be rephrased the "interpersonal intelligences." People with these intelligences are good with other people. They can sense moods, attitudes, intentions, and motivations of others. This intelligence has a high degree of observability and varies widely among boys.

I think you can see that given this list, we might be guilty of being a little snobbish about intelligence. It wanders over a wide range of qualities, and saying that one is better than another is foolish. Each boy has at least one in which he excels. He has at least one in which he lacks talent. Be fair with him.

A Boy's Acting. We can look at a boy's acting in two ways: personal behavior and social behavior.

Curiosity highlights *personal behavior.* This unbridled mental energy makes boys tinker and explore all things. They talk to themselves, try to discover what strange things they can do with their bodies, misuse toys, and pursue a host of other exploration-type activities. Your son is on a constant search for new worlds to understand, and his wiring causes perpetual activity.

Boys must manage a balancing act between strange new things happening inside their small bodies and strange things happening outside with other people. All boys react to this dynamic and confusing situation differently. Their personal intelligences get involved, their fitful and inaccurate ability to think with logic and abstraction gets involved, physical metabolism throws in its wrenches, and of course, there are Mom and Dad to deal with! Any wonder the kids don't know how to act sometimes?

For the most part, *social development* during this phase involves learning social skills such as teamwork, honesty, self-control, and friendship building. "Finding his voice" in the crowd is another element. These developments are rocky roads that bump and bang your boy to exhaustion. It's worsened by the fact that he doesn't understand much of what's going on, and he needs to learn by trial and error. These trials and errors are difficult to grow through, so relax and prepare to be patient.

Prepare yourself also for a long haul. Your son's friendships form and dissolve sometimes within hours. Contention and strife, punctuated with periods of peaceful coexistence with parents and friends, are normal throughout the whole boy range. Telling the truth is a puzzling and tantalizing amusement. Emotional outbursts spontaneously occur, leading to embarrassment and shyness. Boys flirt with various patterns of interaction, testing and trying different "looks" to see how they work and feel. All boys want to be somebody's favorite, and they go to unusual lengths to secure that title. This period is a time of extensive social experimentation. Offer your opinion as frequently as you like. Believe me, your son is looking for ideas of things that work to make friends, fit in, avoid enemies, and have fun.

I must admit total and complete failure at trying to intervene in this process. I've tried to organize "personality swaps" where small groups of boys try acting like someone else in the group. Bad idea. I had boys do visualizations of how they want to act in certain situations. Forget it. I've given boys sheets of paper listing qualities they might want to try out. They made spit wads with them.

You cannot stop this social frenzy as your boy hunts and searches and experiments for a style of behavior he can be comfortable with. You can help this naturally driven search by commenting on the appropriateness or effect of a certain behavior or by merely suggesting new alternatives. He is hopelessly dependent on you for so much, but he is continually experimenting with ways to experience freedom and independence. The best help you can offer is that of a friend and fellow traveler.

A Boy's Feelings. Feelings are a dark mystery for psychology. We don't really know what or why they are, but we know they make us distinctly human. Feelings such as anger and hatred and love are famous and have books written about them. Other feelings—pensiveness and impatience and boredom—aren't cool enough to have their own spots on the bookshelf! Understanding feelings among adults is one notch above pure guesswork, so let's be conservative and realistic with ourselves about understanding our sons.

The most dominating (and ominous) pattern parents see in their boys' emotions is the hiding of emotions over time. This is very normal and usually means nothing more than your boy is gaining self-consciousness, and he feels embarrassed to show publicly what he feels.

I referred earlier to the hump that boys go over around the third and fourth grades. The natural development of self-consciousness is the creator of the hump. Perhaps you remember those initial moments when you knew you were "here." It's a very odd sensation, and most people can recall the strangeness of the experience.

A cloud of ignorance hangs over our understanding of what happens in those moments. We know that as normal brain development proceeds, around the ages of eight to ten we gain sudden flickering perceptions of something new. We can continue to experience the world as we were before, and we also can step outside that and see ourselves as the world sees us. Self-consciousness is a profound event that marks the beginning of adult thinking.

The change affects many areas of behavior. The nature of boyhood shifts noticeably when we pass into self-consciousness. The previous pattern of experimentation continues with this newfound awareness, creating all sorts of new situations. We can suddenly be introspective and wonder to ourselves about important matters of concern, we can read other people's motives and intentions for the first time, and we see ourselves as others see us. It's frightful, interesting, confusing, tantalizing, and inescapable. Boys usually don't talk much about it, but the effects are evident in how they act.

New personality traits might crop up. Periods of quietness and reclusiveness are common. A newfound attention to looks and appearances can be expected. The social patterns of your boy will change.

Another pattern is that of exaggeration of feelings. For the most part, feelings and emotions like intense hatred, joy, courage, despair, jealousy, and many others are being recognized for the first time. Boys tend to play with new things. They do so to varying extremes.

This is why boys of this age are so often referred for counseling. I've talked extensively to teachers who confirm that something very weird happens around the fourth or fifth grade. In my practice, most of the boys referred to me from this age range were expressing normal emotional swings that would subside and integrate into individual personalities over time.

It takes years for a boy to learn to modulate powerful feelings, to use them in socially proper ways, and to learn the fine art of self-control. Until that control develops, his emotions will swerve all over the place. Don't faint; just help him. He's growing up.

Five Hidden Implications of Normal Child Development. You are now combat ready to generally understand your boy. If you did nothing more than ingest this information and mix it up with your intelligent, day-to-day appraisal of your kid, you would be ahead of most parents! But I have found in my work with parents that by encouraging logical conclusions based on this information, parenting boys becomes much more potent.

So, follow me as we walk through some logical conclusions pointing to what you can expect from your son. The first implication is this: *It is your job to be steadfast and unchanging through the swirling waters of boyhood.* Your boys are depending on you to maintain a sensible course in life and model temperance, sensibility, and stability because they have little or none.

I did consulting a few years back with some professional waterskiers. These folks aren't content to stay tucked neatly and safely behind a nice little boat. They slash and bang, looking for wakes to pound, ramps to fly off, and danger to sneer at! They have no sense of fear, no obvious concern for personal safety. They're just like boys. The only thing steady in a water-skier's life is the boat.

Consider yourself the boat your son skis behind. He may act out of control, but he depends on you to stay the course and show him where to go. Your son will go where you pull him.

The second implication is that *it's your part to initiate suggestions for action and movement to higher levels.* Each phase I mentioned previously must be traversed, and leading your son with wisdom and confidence to the next level is essential. He will get through without you, but your help makes the process smoother.

The third implication arises from the fact that *psychology is a young science.* The organized, scientific study of children has been going on for less than seventy-five years. Your observations are as valid as any, and for your child, they may be more accurate than others. Observe your boy; study his sleeping patterns, watch what he eats, and look for connections between disconnected events. Write down what you see and the changes you sense, and draw your own conclusions.

The fourth implication involves the subtle mechanics of brain performance: *Your boy is a solid combination of curiosity, brightness, and distractibility.* Attention spans are very short, and the focus is on the quickly changing sensory landscape. Make your interactions short and concrete, oversimplify your lessons, and prepare yourself for feeling that you're not making a difference!

The fifth implication is that *your presence in your boy's life is significant.* We don't really know how much or how little you need to be present for this natural flow to work properly. Quality or quantity time? It's a moot question. Your boy needs all kinds of time. There is no substitute. It's been said that "80 percent of success is just showing up." Consider this a diamond of wisdom.

Your Attitudes Toward Your Son

Have you ever heard of the Pygmalion effect? This is a famous psychological effect noticed by accident. A certain grad school mixed up the records of high- and low-achieving students, and nobody knew about the mix-up. Low achievers were unknowingly placed with teachers of gifted students, and the gifted kids found themselves with teachers of low achievers.

An amazing thing happened: The below-average performers went through the achievement roof! For perhaps the first time in their lives, a great deal was expected of them. And they worked up to the expectations placed on them by their teacher.

The lesson here should be clear: What you really believe in your heart about your son gets transmitted. What you believe has influential power to form what happens to your son. If you think that he is a worthless loser, he'll know and work toward that level. If you think he is a world-beater, he'll live up to that level.

I heard about a proud mother walking her twin boys in a baby carriage. As she walked down the street, she would stop passersby and announce, "This is David. He's going to be a doctor. This is Michael. He's going to be a lawyer." She annoyed everyone, but she didn't care; she had a vision.

Get a great big positive attitude toward your son! And notice how you communicate that feeling. We communicate our attitudes toward our boys in two versions. The first version is positive: "I want my son to be good with his hands"; "I want my son to be warm and sensitive to women"; "I want my son to be the president of the United States." Positively stated, positively planned, and positively executed.

The second version has a distinctly different sound. It sounds like this: "I just *don't want* my son to be all thumbs"; "I just *don't want* my son to be cold and insensitive to women"; "I just *don't want* my son to be rejected when he runs for office." Notice any differences? Telling him what you *don't want* doesn't tell him what you *do want*. It should be obvious that the first version gives a good target to shoot at; the second gives something bad to be avoided. The differences are worlds apart.

Version one fills you with confidence; version two fills you with a fear of failure. The first gives you a clear way of knowing if you've succeeded; the second never allows you the luxury of knowing if you've been successful or not.

Believe in your boy. Dream big dreams for him; brag about him in front of others; love him and kiss him until he screams. Let him know that you mean to help him reach for the stars!

Imposition of Your Will and Desires

I add this section here for good reasons. Like establishing mission sentences for your son, there is a hairline crack between having big visions for your son and imposing your dreams on him for your satisfaction. This life is his, and you must accept that to operate in his best interests.

You'll never see a better example of the two extremes than the Pinewood Derby. It's a Boy Scout event that has nothing to do with boys. It's for bringing out the worst in men.

There are always two extremes in cars. The first extreme includes those chunks of wood yanked from the box, wheels pounded on, two dunks in what looks like egg drop soup, and off to the races! The other extreme includes the NASA designs, complete with special polymer lacquer finish to reduce wind resistance and special lubricants used only on space shuttle components; they're precision-weighted, radio-controlled, fuel-injected, Dad's-gonna-show-'em, ego-powered pinewood lightning bolts!

The dads of the first group usually don't come to the races (I wouldn't, either), and the dads of the second group arrive with toolboxes. They howl and scream like wounded wookies every time you challenge something about their little ego machines.

Abraham Maslow said, "He who is good with a hammer tends to think everything is a nail." No matter what you are good at, your son should never have to be a nail. If there are things that you want to accomplish in your life, get your own coach, and leave your boy alone!

Lack of Personal / Parental Discipline

This could be your greatest threat to success in this whole journey. It is impossible to ask your son to do something you cannot model for him. He has a large radar dish in his head that hears hypocrisy. If you are unable to discipline yourself to change some aspect of yourself for your betterment, your boy will be unable to see the value in pressing himself, either. Your level of commitment to being your best will become his. Plan and act around this land mine with wisdom and forethought.

Perhaps you are in the unfortunate situation where all your habits are well-structured and in control, but those of other adults in your son's life are not. Estranged spouses, grandparents, neighbors, and others can exert undue and confusing influence. I offer a suggestion that I know is easier to say than to accomplish. You must apply your level-best effort to align all the adults in your boy's life in the same direction. To the best of your ability, get people to change bad or contradictory habits.

I worked with a divorced couple who had five young kids. It was a very sad situation. The husband smoked marijuana, and he thought it was fine to do so in front of the children. Mom was quite the sharper of the two, and naturally, she thought his idea stank. She was right. The fellow was willing to talk reasonably, and the conversation we had illuminates some useful points in gaining the help of people engaging in destructive modeling.

The father thought that pot should be legal. He didn't think that pot was harmful to his health. He didn't think that pot made him less productive.

"What," I asked, "does pot do for you?"

"It helps me get through," he replied.

"Is pot taking you where you want to go?" I asked.

No reply. He was much smarter than I thought because the answer was obviously no.

"Do you think that pot will help your kids get where they want to go?" I asked.

Again, no reply. I was starting to like the guy. It is so instructive to remember that all parents have maternal and paternal instincts deep inside them. Tapping those feelings and urges takes good questions.

"Do you want to help your kids get where they want to go?" I asked after some time.

"Yes, of course," he answered.

"Then help them," I said.

He never smoked in front of them again.

I NEED TO TELL YOU SOME FACTS OF LIFE

I have listed things that pose threats to your success in raising a winner. You should review the list often. But I have discovered something very interesting about parents.

Parents are relieved to learn that what they tussle and struggle with is exactly what other parents struggle with too! They don't feel so alone then. You are not alone! The normal problems to be expected by us all are what to consider the facts of life. And we need to face these facts with clear eyes and realistic expectations.

Fact of Life #1: Boys Are by Nature Inattentive and Ungrateful

They need to learn these graces over time, and with some assistance (reminding), they do. I know parents get irritated with ungrateful or frightfully flaky sons. Be patient, though; your boy will come around. Give him time.

Fact of Life #2: Life Has a Leveling Action

No matter how strange or bizarre or dysfunctional your son may seem at times, he will show at some time an equal amount of positive behavior. You might not be around to see it, but it will happen.

In science there is a concept called *regression*. It suggests that there are average amounts of behavior that people are likely to do: an average amount of hair combing each day, an average amount of crying, an average amount of sweating, and so on. Everything has an average.

Regression says that people tend to hover around their personal averages on any one behavior and return to it quickly if they deviate. Let's say there is an average number of times you say, "I love you," each day. If your average is 4 times per day, there is a high likelihood that you won't deviate from that number. If you do, there is a high probability that you will return to your average quickly. If on one day you don't say it at all, there is a good chance that the next day you will say it four times. If on one day you say it 150 times, chances are good that the next day you will say it 4 times.

If your boy does something really odd (and he will), you can expect normal behavior to follow. The problem may be that you will be too busy reeling backward about the bad stuff to notice the good stuff! Get your balance and start looking. Good usually follows bad, and bad usually follows good.

Fact of Life #3: There Are Few Meaningful Averages in Behavior

Is your boy average? Well, I hope so, but I must tell you that average happens over a suspiciously large area. Is there an average amount of crying boys do? Of course, there is an average. Is it important or informative? No! You might feel that if you have a sense of what is normal and what isn't you ought to trust that feeling. You will find that the most interesting aspects of your son are outside the realm of averages. Can he love? Does he have a developing sense of character, right and wrong, fairness? Many things are beyond the artificial sensibility of statistical averages. Concern yourself with whether your boy is exceptional.

Fact of Life #4: Statistically Speaking, 25 Percent of Everything Boys Do Is Extreme

Think about the word *extreme*. If your boy does one hundred things per day, twenty-five of them will be extreme for him. It's as predictable as the seasons. In my counseling practice, I always tried to reassure parents of this fact by pointing out that no matter how good Junior was, a large chunk of behavior had to be bad! Boys cannot be good all the time.

Now, your boy can't be a complete outlaw or a complete angel. He bounces around in between with terrific predictability. Prepare for this ahead of time and save yourself some broken expectations.

Fact of Life #5: Boys Beg for Direction and Guidelines

They ask for direction and guidance in strange ways. Research indicates that boys feel neglected if somewhat strict guidelines and performance standards aren't expected. They have a sense of security to know that external sources of final authority have control. Relax the guidelines, and your boy will react by forcing you to enact more! Boys are not happy doing their own thing or being totally free. Give your boy what he is asking for.

Fact of Life #6: Identities Will Emerge from Your Boy That You Don't Know

Get ready for Jekyll and Hyde. We reviewed the extent to which boys experiment with things, personalities and identities included. Strange personalities come and go. Let them float on through, for usually boys end up embarrassed by them, dropping them like hot potatoes, often as fast as they put them on.

Fact of Life #7: What's Well-Adjusted Changes with the Wind

The world's standard of what is well-adjusted fluctuates wildly. Some 90 to 95 percent of boys are perfectly normal and well-adjusted.

Parents hear about the latest "abnormal" things and run home to observe Johnny. The fringe element gains far too much press.

Balance yourself against the fringe. Invest some time in honest thinking about what you believe to be well adjusted. Stimulate your thoughts by seeking the wise counsel of people you trust. A perspective born of these activities will have more balance, depth, and credibility than anything the world will offer. Think for yourself and trust in it.

Fact of Life #8: Your Boy Is Going to Break Your Heart

He's going to surprise you; he's going to run from you; he'll spurn you in ways that will be very painful. I'll never forget the day I first saw this reality with my boys. It was the day we talked about swearing.

We spoke very candidly about each word, and I let the boys say each one in front of me. We had a frank discussion about what the swear words meant and why using them was not proper. And as I walked away after the conversation, I knew that an innocent part of my boys was gone forever.

Fact of Life #9: Your Boy Didn't Choose to Be Who He Is

I have a copy of Og Mandino's book *The Greatest Miracle in the World*. It's a timeless little book full of courage and love for things in life that really count. I enjoyed giving away copies to my young counselees because there is a section that talks about how each of us is the greatest miracle in the world.

I read that to young kids coming to see me, and they often acted as if they'd never been told what a miracle they were. In all their uniqueness, in all their thoughts and dreams, each of them was one of a kind. Many of them had never been talked to that way. Each boy knew only he was one of a kind all right! The bad kind.

Your boy is beginning to realize some things about himself that you have known for a long time. He was born with traits and qualities that neither of you chose but that both of you must live with. You might deeply wish that he were different from the way he is. He might wish he were different. Either way, accept him, and commit to being the best parent you can be to him as he is.

Fact of Life #10: "With My Dying Breath . . ."

One night I was having a long bedtime chat with my kids. I had told them that I would love them no matter what they ever did, and I would stand by and support them forever. Zac was busy thinking of the worst thing he could do. After running through stealing, fighting, and telling lies, he thought of the "absolute worst thing: What if I shot you with a gun?" The other kids gasped. "With my dying breath," I slowly said, "I would say that I love you, Zac."

He was quiet for a long time, and then said, "That's a pretty good deal, Dad!"

A little bit later, my older son, Jake, took me aside and asked me if I was serious. "Of course, I'm serious, Jake. There is nothing in the world that could make me not love you." He was stunned. I tell this kid all the time that I love him, and he still didn't believe it!

Your boy needs constant reassurance of your love, support, and end-less forgiveness. These qualities don't normally compute in a boy's head, so he forgets and needs to be reminded often.

Fact of Life #11: Everything's Gonna Be Just Fine!

Norman Cousins tells of a time he was at a football game, and an emer-gency squad gathered around a guy lying on the ground, the victim of an apparent heart attack. The guy lay still—dazed, confused, and pale with fear. The emergency personnel were hustling around, proficiently doing their jobs, but Cousins noticed that nobody was talking to the man.

Acting on instinct, Cousins coolly strode up to the quivering fellow and placed his hand on the man's shoulder. He warmly looked the guy in the eye and said, "You know, mister, this emergency squad is the best

I have ever seen. They are the most well-trained and best-equipped group you could have possibly gotten. They know exactly what they are doing, and you can rest assured that you are getting the finest care available. Everything's gonna be fine!"

Everything's gonna be just fine. Lots of people have survived boyhood and so will you!

ACTION TO TAKE

You can begin now. This chapter has presented you with sufficient background to move forward. Let's look at the process of how to develop the traits typical to Renaissance men.

CHAPTER 6

BoyThink: Rifles, Lizards, and Monsters

Youth is a wonderful thing. What a crime to waste it all on children.

—*George Bernard Shaw*

 How and what boys think appears to be a mystery. Mastering some simple truths makes deciphering this puzzle much easier.

WALK A MILE IN MY SHOES

I am a Cub Scout pack leader, and I also lead a smaller group of boys called a den. When I first started as a den leader, I had grandiose plans to bestow my ageless wisdom upon the young American men. I thought I'd be really good for them.

The Cub Scout handbook had pictures of clean-cut, happy boys, all standing around in a circle with their perfect little uniforms, respectfully saluting the flag. *Ain't this just America?* I thought.

Talk about a misleading image of a group! You should have seen my boys! They were a ragtag bunch capable of only two things: eating and running (their legs and their mouths). In our first meeting, I intended to teach them to "grow up to be distinguished citizens and to carry forth the principles and duties set out before us by our forefathers . . ." but these boys were looking at each other and crinkling up their noses. I decided I'd better shift gears fast.

"Okay, girls," I said.

All whispering stopped. All eyes turned beady; nostrils flared in bitter anger.

"What would you like to talk about if we don't talk about good citizenship?"

It worked. Their eyes lit up, and they started to pour out the most fun things. "Let's talk about rifles," said the little huntsman to my left. "No, I want talk about lizards," said the little adventurer sitting off to my right. "No, NO!" shouted a third. "Let's talk about monsters!" "Yeah, MONSTERS!" they shrieked in unison.

Every eye in the room was on fire! Every mind ignited with horror and screams and goose bumps! They were all instantly caught up in the monster frenzy, and all I could do was watch as the minidrama exploded. It stunned me. Almost no prompting at all and—WHOOSH!—away they went, creating things much more interesting than anything I thought up.

Well, the night went pretty well after that as we started to talk about famous monsters and boring monsters. Somehow the time passed, and the kids learned about good monster citizens.

DR. FREUD VS. DR. SEUSS

Those boys taught me a lot that night. Real life is a classroom, and I get a new lesson in street psychology every Cub Scout night.

Boys are not like adults. They perceive situations and people differently, their understanding of power and social positioning is foreign to us, and they think at levels we've long since outgrown. All that combines to make understanding boyhood joyfully difficult. But you'll never have more fun getting practically nowhere!

I'll ask you an intriguing question: Who understands boys better, Freud or Seuss? Your answer probably says a great deal about how you'll approach understanding your son. My mind says, "Science must have some answers," but my heart is chanting, "Green eggs and ham!"

How many ways can we analyze boys? We can gather endless knowledge about boys, but understanding them is a radically different matter. Knowledge is recognizing habits and tendencies, weak points, strong points, and other similar kinds of information. Understanding, however, comes from firsthand insight into motives, knowing how all the pieces of information fit together, and having a feel for what it's like.

Understanding boyhood must come from personal experience. Secretly, we're all anxious to reach back and grab for that wonderful feeling. Movie moguls and Madison Avenue executives recognize this. They tempt us with entertainment, movies, and ads that glorify boyhood and the magic of being young again. But childhood always seems slightly out of reach, a little too far back in the fuzzy past. A little taste would be so delicious! It might even help us as parents.

The best way to raise your boy is probably to become a better boy yourself. You cannot in all likelihood learn it, so you must relive it. You can really understand only after you have again frolicked and played in that crazy universe called boyhood or allowed yourself to remember that far-off time when anything was possible.

And what if you're female? Don't you think you're automatically dismissed? Though I don't think you can really know what being a boy was like, you certainly have enough experience with childhood to get the general idea. If you apply yourself to re-create the essence of childhood, you will be doing your son a remarkable favor. Besides, it's a blast.

But These Shoes Don't Fit Like They Used To

We are going to find out what it's like to be a boy in a very unusual way. Let's not interview boys because I've already done that. Feel free to try; I had fun trying in vain! As I began writing this book, I conducted a series of interviews with boys to ask them some pointed questions. I told them that I was writing a book about them, and I needed them to tell me something important about boyhood. I had a hard time getting straight answers (we do want straight answers, don't we?), but I sure laughed a lot!

One little fellow said, "It's a great honor to be a boy because . . . that means I don't have to have babies." Another one said, "I love being a boy because who would want to be a girl or a donkey?" Boys understand life on such a simple level.

What's the worst crime a boy can commit? I heard answers ranging from having sex in cars to killing cats to stealing fossils from the local park.

Collectively, the group thought that "old" was early thirties and that parents didn't really know what life was about. Doesn't every generation think it's the enlightened one?

Though the twenty-first century has cultural challenges of its own, all of us have shared childhood. Can any of the magic of our childhoods be relived? Can we reacquire it in some way? Oh, to understand life the way these little minds do. It would be a great treat.

In the early 1500s, Juan Ponce de Leon scoured the Caribbean looking for a fountain the native people said rejuvenated those who bathed in it. Your boy has found that fountain of youth and bathes in it every day. You may join him if you choose. Becoming a boy again forms the foundation of a very special friendship.

Let's go through two phases to learn about how boys think. First, let's have some fun with the following list of experiences you share in common with your son, but you probably hadn't thought about. Find a quiet spot, read the list item by item, and stop to let your mind drift after each. Let your mind wander. That's what boys do.

- Present wrapped up with a bow
- Worms
- Hot summer days
- Pulling weeds
- Ice cream
- Pickup baseball games
- Summer camp
- Thunderstorms
- Basements
- Noises at night
- Feeling like you got away with something naughty
- Five pieces of gum at once
- Stepping in the muck at the bottom of a pond
- Snowball fights
- Walking to school
- Your first-grade classroom
- Your favorite spot in your home
- The safety of your mother's or father's arms
- Grandma's and Grandpa's house

Your brain is strewn with thousands of memories such as these. Most of them are in shards and scraps, and so you don't remember them as well as you will recognize them. That is why with some prompting like this exercise, you can easily retrieve specific memories.

BoyThink: The Normal Boy's Obsessions

As adults, we've rushed far away from the real texture of childhood. The effects of this movement make it harder and harder to relate to what our kids are going through. We don't "get it" like they do, and we frankly are of little use to them if we remain insensitive to how they operate. Where there is no basis for commonality, vital connections between our boys and us erode, and unity stops. Nobody wants to be an impotent parent, particularly if you have a commitment to be exceptional.

Let me illustrate this difference. I gave a talk to a small group of parents about the simplicity of childlike thinking. I taught them the child's game of paper, scissors, and rock. Most of them remembered the rules well. I recommended that they play this game with their children for no reason. Well, they needed some more information about childlike logic, perception, and implied meanings in conversations, self-esteem, and so on. To my amazement, nobody asked me how to have more fun with this game!

I followed up some weeks later with a few members of the group. I shouldn't have been shocked, but they had more questions and queries. What was worse, none of them had gone home and played the dumb game. In moments like that, I feel we as adults have lost something vital.

I want to give you some information that will help you think about how boys think. BoyThink consists of four major elements:

1. Boys are sensory captive.

2. Boys are highly instinctual.

3. Immense curiosity shortens attention spans to seconds.

4. The world is black or white.

By *sensory captive*, I mean that boys live in a world confined to what they can see and hear and touch and smell and taste. This is very different from the way you operate. Until the onset of self-consciousness, they understand the world by looking, sniffing, grabbing, biting, and poking. They are not thinking nearly as much as collecting information. Even after the transition, boys tend to focus on body noises, squirmy animals, breaking glass—anything that excites the senses. Sounds primitive, huh?

By *highly instinctual*, I mean that boys do not operate from a position of automatic logic (as we adults do) as much as by intuitive feel. Where brainpower is absent, instincts dominate. Boys are very conscious of people and events around them, but they respond quickly to feelings of intimidation, power, pecking orders, and territoriality. Their instincts are not subject to thoughts like an adult's are; rather, they have built-in defensive and offensive schemes that enable them to act in the world. This is one key reason some kids can grow up more or less normal in the most adverse situations imaginable.

Boys' *attention spans* are controlled by curiosity and are at the mercy of salient sensory stimulation. That's a Harvard way of saying they pay attention to the most noticeable things around them. Curiosity is the cognitive force behind short attention spans. Boys must learn over time to ignore extraneous activities going on around them and focus on one thing. Nature has wired them mentally to latch on to things that move and sparkle and dazzle. Boys are controlled by these forces. You as a seasoned and focused adult may be unable to appreciate your boy's difficulty in channeling these forces.

By *black or white*, I mean that boys learn only by experience that there are gradations between qualities such as good and bad, right and wrong, love and hate. To them, life is either/or; no in between. For example, until a boy gets to the eight- to ten-year-old range, he is puzzled about your ability to love him and be mad at him at the same time. For a boy, those two cannot exist at the same time! Is it any wonder that so many boys feel confused?

A NORMAL BOY'S NEEDS

The Children's Defense Fund considers the four elementary needs of children to be (1) a need to feel wanted and accepted, (2) a need for continuity in relationships, (3) a need to have some sense that there is a regular, dependable quality to the world in which they live, and (4) a need for thoughtful guidance in coping with the demands of growing up.

This is an excellent list, but keep in mind that rigid application of this or any other list can cause problems. Think about how you might try to meet these needs in your son, and you will recognize potential difficulties. For example, your boy needs your thoughtful guidance but is also naturally driven by high levels of spontaneity and curiosity. Get ready! He needs a sense of regularity and dependability, yet he is highly instinctual. Prepare yourself!

Boys frequently spit in the wind, bite the hand that feeds them, and say they hate people they like! Natural qualities of boys can be difficult to handle. Because of the continual "trouble" that some boys create, we might conclude we are better off leaving them alone. Don't kid yourself.

The reason I highlight this problem now is that you are the sum total of all your yesterdays. All your experiences and thoughts combined brought you to this instant in time. That you have arrived here with any degree of normalcy indicates your parents or caretakers must have done something right. Whether you remember these right things is immaterial. The fact remains that they had to have met some basic needs. If those people met them for you, you can meet them for your son.

You'll find phase two of our retrospective to be very different from the first. I again want you to find a quiet space and consider the following list. I want you to keep in mind any one of the four factors of BoyThink.

If you choose to approach one of these experiences in a sensory-bound way, try not to think about the experience; relive what you saw, heard, tasted, smelled, and felt. Allow yourself to be filled with the immense joy of sensing. Lose your mind and come to your senses.

If you choose to be instinctual, become aware of your feel of the situation. Try if you can to imagine what an animal would feel. Recall the feelings of being power conscious and absorbed with survival.

If you are going to focus on attention span, notice how easy it is to flit from one thought and focal point to another. You should clearly feel the energy-rich excitement of life and the fresh, captivating nature of everything around you.

The black-or-white, either/or element is probably the most difficult to apply. To boys, this element is very pronounced, so appreciate the terrific learning value for you in doing it well.

Using the key phrases in this list, go back and recall those moments. Maintain the perspective that two opposite things cannot be true at the same time. Notice how that feels.

- Catching a baby animal

- Pets

- Dead pets

- The smell of worms after a storm

- Having a neighbor get mad at you

- Saying something really mean to someone

- Hearing something very strange

- Your best friend

- Hearing Mom and Dad fight

- Sleeping outside

- Cloudy days

- Wanting to fly

- The silence of being under water

- Baseball cards

- No money

- Bullies

- Wanting to hide

- Santa Claus

- Church pews

- Bad dreams

- Fire

Phase two is much more boylike than phase one. You became more of a boy in this experience. Remember, this is a knowledge of boyhood, not an understanding. Knowledge is in the head; understanding is in action.

You will recall my saying that teaching a boy involves becoming a better boy yourself. I want you to do a few things that boys would do. This activity might be embarrassing, it might be uncomfortable, and it might seem silly; the more you feel any of these, the farther out of touch with boyhood you are. If you don't believe me, ask your son.

Try any of these and like them:

- Walk in the mud with no shoes.

- Walk anywhere with no shoes.

- Fly a kite.

- Hide in the bushes.

- Ambush your children.

- Challenge your boy to a footrace.

- Skip (in private if necessary).

- Honk and wave at perfect strangers.

- Buy a kazoo and learn to play it.

- Do something you've been warned *not* to do.

- Learn a magic trick.

- Teach yourself to juggle.

Wringing life out of life is something boys do routinely. They don't know any different. They don't know many boundaries, and they are free to be led by curiosities and impulses. Understanding boyhood requires that you know that feeling. Let yourself go and understand the magic.

LAUGH!

The first thing a man does when asked about boyhood is smile. Try it. Somebody once said that children and fools cannot lie, so the smiles must mean something. In *The Adolescent,* Fyodor Dostoyevsky wrote,

If you wish to glimpse inside a human soul and get to know a man, don't bother analyzing his ways of being silent, of talking, of weeping, or seeing how much he is moved by noble ideas; you'll get better results if you just watch him laugh. If he laughs well, he is a good man.

All I claim to know is that laughter is the most reliable gauge of human nature. Look at children for instance: Children are the only human creatures to produce perfect laughter and that's what makes them so enchanting.

I can rarely go past a playground without stopping to roll down the window and listen. The sounds are pure and joyful. Little voices that have those sparkling laughs somehow infect me. We need to laugh a lot more, and to share this laughter with our children. Magic happens interpersonally when you share belly laughs with your boy. I can't explain it, yet I am sure beyond a doubt that laughter is one of the sources of emotional bonding and happiness.

DID YOUR PARENTS MEET THE NINE CRITERIA OF GOOD PARENTS?

Your parents or caretakers did something right. Unless you're forced by your spouse at gunpoint to read this book, you've got a drive to understand your son better and be better. That's no accident. Where did that drive come from?

Somewhere in your yesterdays. Whether your life has been a bowl of cherries or a bowl of tears makes no difference. You are a parent who thrives. I have made it clear that understanding boyhood requires being a child again. If you could go back into childhood, you would find certain things happening within you to develop this thriving for life. What might they be?

In Vance Packard's 1983 book *Our Endangered Children,* he suggests nine skills good parents use to create an environment where kids thrive.

1. Skillful child-developers make it clear that they are crazy about that particular child. Somebody in your life must have been crazy about you. Figure out who it was and what the person did to make you know you were special.

2. Skillful child-developers do much interacting, especially verbal, with the child. Who talked to you? What did they want to know? Who did you especially like talking with? How did it make you feel when you knew others wanted to speak with you?

3. Skillful child-developers work to help the child develop a high level of self-esteem. Don't get too hung up on the word *self-esteem*. Who respected you, paid attention to you, and generally told you that you had value?

4. Skillful child-developers condition children to do well. Somehow, somewhere you must have been rewarded for doing well, even if the reward was from you to yourself. Recall some experiences of this.

5. Expert child-developers encourage children to be explorers. Did you feel the freedom to move out and explore as a kid? At what point did you know that you wanted to know more and begin actively to search your environment? Who encouraged it?

6. Good parents try to give their children a sense of family solidarity (even in single-parent homes). Spending time together, talking to one another, uniting to solve problems, making decisions together, and playing together are some qualities of solidarity you might search for.

7. Skillfull child-builders are good at moving children from parental discipline to self-discipline. You've taken it upon yourself to be a searcher and learner. That is classic self-discipline. Where did it come from? When did you learn it? Who helped you develop it, and how did they do it?

8. Skillful parents guide their children to a clear set of values. It's no exaggeration that values among adults are more like Jell-O Jigglers than granite edifices. Many adults really don't claim to support any overarching set of values or codes or standards. They seem more driven by self-enhancement or immediate pleasure. If this description fits you, search around yourself to find out if anyone in your past anchored you to any moral code or value that stuck with you. See if that value persists in your life, and observe how it has helped or harmed you.

9. Expert child-raisers help their children experience plenty of responsibility. Who gave you jobs to do? Who monitored your progress and showed you how to do chores? Who was responsible for your responsibility?

Feel free to apply these ideas to your boy if you like. Some of them must have been a centerpiece of your childhood. Remember exactly how they made you feel, and understand that your son wants to feel the same things. Understand what it means to be a boy again!

ACTION TO TAKE

The main purpose of this chapter is to guide you through the files of your childhood. Crazy as that may sound, firsthand experience in childhood is something you have; you just don't remember enough of it to relate powerfully to your boy. To walk as he walks, see and talk as he sees and talks, and feel it all over again place immense power in his hands. Powerful rapport is of major significance in building a winner. Use this chapter to recall what you already know!

CHAPTER 7

Wrestle-lationships

Boys communicate very little through verbal channels. Communicating with boys for understanding comes with the application of a different approach. Talk with your touch.

A FEEDING FRENZY

Every once in awhile, I'll growl at my kids like a mean old dog. I don't say anything. I just slowly squint my eyes, curl the corner of my lip, and spit this raspy snarl toward them. They love it because it means something special to them. Playtime has come.

They know that for the next half hour they have me, rolling on the ground, tickling, pinching, and tossing. I can't think of anything that they love more.

It always surprises me that after these sessions, the kids scream for more. It's like they've been feeding this insatiable hunger and don't want to be told it's time to stop. Though rolled, tickled, and creamed, they still love it!

Your Son Doesn't Know That He Needs a Relationship

If you'll recall what we discussed earlier, until your son emerges from that moment in life when he gains self-consciousness, he can't even know that he's here! Prior to that time, he shares your space, but he is completely unaware of the nature of the bond linking you. All he knows is that you are there and he wants you to stay there.

But he maintains a strange urge. His emotions are steering him to get close to you. He doesn't understand intellectually what's happening; he knows only that he wants physical closeness. This drive is responsible for many behaviors. Nuzzling, touching, sitting on your lap, and holding hands are examples. To your son, they are life.

A boy needs to be touched. He will do almost anything to get touched. For him, it is the prime expression of love and attention, and without it, he feels neglected and unloved. This force is built in for good reasons, and you must be alert to its presence.

A boy asks for contact constantly, but his requests are nonverbal. He wants you to put down the paper and look at him when he speaks. He wants to hold hands and sit on your lap. He wants hugs. He wants you to sit next to him at the table. He wants you to play and wrestle and tousle his hair. He wants to feel your arms around him. To your boy, these are thousands of times more meaningful than sterile "I love you's" thrown around like dog bones.

He wants to give touches too. Think about this: Wouldn't it make sense that the best way he has to tell you he loves you is through touch? For adults, a relationship builds and reinforces a deeper bond between two unbonded people. A relationship is a two-way street. If carefully nurtured, it grows into a bond greater than the sum of the interactions between the two.

Your boy feels bonded to you naturally, and his prime urge is to express the joy and sense of happiness he feels when he is around you. A parent-child relationship is the most special connection you can ever have with another human being.

Do you realize how blessed you are to have a son? He wants to be close to you, and though he can't give you much else, his personal contact is the best he has to offer. There is a special way you can honor that effort: Return it.

How?

I have studied and puzzled over this relationship riddle for a long time. Relationships seem to be made-up pieces that fit together like a patchwork quilt. But I sense there's much more to it than that. Good relationships have a mystical quality about them.

Can the special mystery of a good relationship with your boy be created on purpose? Of course, but it must happen unconventionally. Creating a relationship that builds a Renaissance man depends on building a good relationship that a little boy understands. Creating a Renaissance man is an ambitious undertaking. It won't happen by some gee-whiz space-age technology. It won't happen through psychology or drum beating or chemistry. The magic of the human connection occurs between two people: you and your son.

The hows of an unconventional approach break down into three steps. First, gain rapport through playfulness; second, challenge unspoken relational rules; and third, reach out and touch him.

You need to be inspired to display your unique playfulness. Teaching is the introduction of new information; inspiration is bringing out the stuff that is already inside you. Learn this difference. Playfulness, fun-lovingness, joy, and lightheartedness must spring from you. These qualities are inside, no matter how drab you may feel. Playfulness forms a special kind of rapport that builds relationships of change.

In the last chapter, we created some ability to enhance your memories of childhood. The purpose was to provide for you a look at childhood from a kid's perspective. The experience of childhood has not substantially changed for thousands of years. Therefore, spending time developing your memory of childhood can provide a new perspective on what your child is going through today. That understanding is the first step toward gaining rapport. Let's put that understanding to work.

I've Got a Secret

You don't really need to know a thing to be a superb boy relater. You need to be willing to take the first step and roll up your sleeves, let down your hair, and play in the dirt. If you have a bulletproof ego, you'll have a blast! Your boy will be agog when he sees you lower yourself to his level, and that's the start of solid rapport.

Relationships Have Unspoken Rules

We obey unspoken rules. These rules apply not only in relationships with other people but also in every sort of social setting. You know the pressure you feel to perform, to do and not do certain things in certain settings? When I was dating my wife, Kathi, there were some specific rules of conduct that I observed when I was with her parents that I didn't have to observe when we were alone. That is, not as long as I valued my life! Among coworkers, for instance, you might feel pressure to act or dress or talk in a certain way that you wouldn't feel with a close friend. Nobody, mind you, insists that you act or dress or talk a certain way, but you feel as though if you don't, you're breaking a rule.

There's a strange thing about these rules. We voluntarily treat them as though they're etched in granite. Inside relationships, clusters of rules exist surreptitiously. Your relationships are under the direct influence of secret forces you don't control. You obey these hidden rules by acting in ways you *think* the relationship demands that you act.

I once had the chance to watch a group of boys I know through a one-way mirror. They didn't know I was there, and they were laughing and carrying on, speaking about things I didn't think they knew. Their interactions were so foreign to me, I hardly recognized them. They were operating under a completely different set of rules from what they would if I were present.

Now, what do you think would have happened if I had walked into the room? They would have shifted gears quickly to adapt to the rules that go into effect when Bill is around. We didn't decide on these rules. These boys created them, and they live by them whether I want them to or not. The boys feel the need to follow them meticulously and do so with regularity.

Relationships among people grow and change only if the unspoken rules are challenged and changed. If unchallenged, the unspoken rules will overcontrol you right into stagnation and boredom. They have the ability to choke off relationships. The only way to change your relationships with others is to find out what the rules are and challenge them directly.

On occasion our family has what I call "open forum." That means the kids can do and say anything without fear of reprisal or humiliation. The kids could do that anytime anyway, but they don't believe it. They operate with a rule that says, "If you're honest about something Mom and Dad think is bad, you'll be in big trouble." They act as though this is true. The open forum allows them to safely skirt this rule and fearlessly tell us what they are really thinking. It's very freeing for them and eye-opening for us.

Effectively dealing with rules lies at the heart of gaining rapport with your boy. Every relationship has rules for gaining rapport. That means for every person you do or don't know, there's a set pattern of words and actions you allow yourself to use to make contact. Nothing is stopping you from acting any way you choose, except the rules you choose to perform by.

What does this mean for you and your son? It means that better rapport between you two can grow from challenging whatever rules you sense are stifling you. How do you challenge them?

When you feel that you must act a certain way with him, quickly do the opposite. If you feel that you must say, "Good morning, Charlie," you could challenge the rule by grabbing him and throwing him to the ground and kissing him on the lips! That would be a delicate bend of the rule, no? Impulsively react to stifling rules when you feel them.

These things you do to challenge the flow are going to have a jarring effect on your boy. That jarring is usually good and momentarily opens both of you to vast new frontiers of friendship. The moment you have challenged the rules, you can for a short moment do anything you want because your action suspends all the rules.

Don't make your bond with your son bondage for you both. Use this as a rule of thumb: Be spontaneous at any instant you feel as though you are plodding through the normal interactions with your kid. Jump up and do something different. This has the effect of bending and stretching and bringing forth a fresh flexibility into your bond.

Building Bridges

Several years ago, AT&T hired a consulting firm to create a slogan that would capture the world. All possible approaches were considered, and no expense was spared. The final product was simple and revealing. Did you ever feel that you should "reach out and touch someone"?

There is magic in the human touch. It's a universal human experience that crosses ages, generations, cultures. From the gentlest brush to a thundering slap to a warm caress and on and on, a touch is worth a million words.

People touch in many ways. You've felt a warm glance, a cold stare, and been tongue-lashed. You've given gentle encouragement with a kind voice. You've dealt harsh blows with a deadly glare and fiery squeeze of the hand. Touching someone is a remarkable jungle of activity and understanding.

Touchless Ways to Touch

You can see that you don't have to actually touch your son to touch him. To learn this fine and delicate art, try a few of these suggestions.

- Stare at him without a word.
- Wear some cologne that he likes.
- Make him smell something you smell.
- Put a surprise somewhere and tell him where to find it.
- Put a worm in his bed.
- Put a friendly note in his lunch box.
- Name a tree after him.
- Ask his opinion.
- Make him a special meal.
- Glare at him.
- Repeat his exact words after he speaks.
- Imitate him.
- Build him something with your hands.
- Put a Post-it note on his toothbrush.
- Put out a totally mismatched set of clothes for him.
- Read a story to him.
- Put a place card at his place at the dinner table.
- Put stones in his shoes and deny any knowledge of it.
- Put a "Welcome Home" banner on the house after school.

- Make up a song about him and sing it to him.

- Say a poem with his name in it.

- Draw a picture of you and your son doing something fun.

- Unplug the TV and tell him you are the entertainment for the night.

- Split a large bag of M&M's with him right before dinner.

- Take him to work for the day.

- Give him an autographed picture of you.

- Write messages on the windows with dry-erase markers.

- Put messages on trees along the path to school.

- Drop all you are doing and listen to him.

This list can be as long as there is creativity. What counts is that each action touches your boy. Each touch gives him substance, verifies his presence and value, and makes him feel set apart and special. You are building a relational foundation that will last forever.

Now You Need a Wrestle-lationship

As you've probably noticed, my general inclination is to shun academic explanations of certain matters and cut straight to the meat. Ockham's razor, you know. You now have the required background to know the *why* of what I am about to share, so I trust you are with me and are ready to eat a large feast of effectiveness.

Boys are not generally reserved or gentle. Just look at their sneakers and pants for goodness' sake! Dirt and holes! They understand rough and tumble, and that is precisely how you should approach them.

I mentioned the terrific importance of touch and the need for you to know the various ways to make physical contact. Allow me to make a short list:

- Punch and poke.

- Pinch and grab.

- Hug and tickle.

- Kiss and twist.

- Pet and scratch.

- Hold hands and carry him.

- Wrestle and tussle.

I suspect some elaboration is in order. Punch and poke gently. Pinch and grab quickly and unexpectedly. Hug and tickle with no forewarning and with complete abandon. Twist the cheeks and ears. Pet him on the head, and scratch him on the back. Grab his self-conscious hands, and swoop him up into your arms. Dive on the floor and mess up his hair. Do this all in happiness and love!

The goal here is to make contact, not to hurt him. I've seen so many people of a softer persuasion sneer as I've mentioned this list. We live in an age of child-abuse awareness, and I am clear about the images conjured by this list. Placed within the context of hatred, these suggestions sound brutal. In the context of love and fun, this list constitutes the most natural play parents and boys can enjoy.

You probably play like this with your boy anyway. If it's totally foreign to you, start slowly and build up activity, as you feel more comfortable. If you've never done any of these things with your son, he might be a little annoyed at the whole proposition. I promise, though, that he will warm up to it quickly.

And another caveat: I have seen a few boys who for whatever reason hate the idea of physical contact like the methods I'm describing. Particularly around the third and fourth grades, boys start to shun physical contact because of the way it looks. They still need to be touched, but they will put up "manly" resistance. I usually attack these little ice cubes with everything I've got!

The point is to make contact that your boy understands—a bridge by which your lives become verifiably connected. That bridge provides a way for the relationship to expand into other areas over the course of your mutual lifetimes. The only mistake you can make is no attempt at all.

AGITATE, AGITATE, AND AGITATE

When my kids were fairly young, they—and the hordes of friends they brought home—taught me more about life in a zoo than I really wanted to know.

One of the major lessons I noticed early is that kids love to be agitated. They love for you to be playful, to play tricks ("gig" them as we call it at home), to do cool stuff like high fives, secret handshakes, NFL end-zone dances, winking, and so on. Sneak attacks work well too, with no holds barred. They love it when you force the action, make them respond, and get in their faces in an unmistakable way.

You may kid them as well: "Hey, the neighbors tell me you're Superman. Can I touch your cape?" Sometimes I told the children in the neighborhood that they had to pay me ten dollars to play with my kids. If they didn't have cash, I put it on their tab. Believe me, I lay awake at night thinking up new ways to gig them, always looking for good ideas, and continually listening for good lines to use with kids. I'm addicted to challenging the rules.

As I write this section, I remember a particular gig my son Zac and his friend did several years ago. Zac yelled from downstairs that he had "something fun for me to see." His voice sounded a little funny, and I suspected a gig.

As I came down the stairs, they burst out from behind the furniture like Butch and Sundance, and they soaked me with water guns. Of course, I had to grab them and wrestle the little aqua guerrillas to the carpet. Don't they know we have a rule about water guns in the house? I showed them who's boss, eh?

Your son will quickly grow accustomed to these sorts of activities I've talked about. When he feels a connection to you, a strange thing will start to happen. He will begin to dish it back. You may or may not like it, so get ready. It means something special.

It's called rapport. You see, a relationship becomes a two-way street when rapport becomes two-way. The time will come when he gigs you. Remember that he was thinking about you when you weren't there. He was probably a little afraid to try it, and it took guts. Remember that he cares about you. Try not to blow your stack!

Congratulations! You're having a relationship.

INCH BY INCH, ROW BY ROW

Building a Renaissance man takes time. I've observed an immutable law of the universe that nothing of any value happens quickly. The slowness of the development has a distinct pattern. You surge forward, then have setbacks, then forward a few more steps, then reversals again. Life has this forward-backward characteristic that nobody escapes. Your relationship with your son will not be born in one interaction that goes well. It will not die in one, two, or ten thousand that go bad. You can expect many victories and many defeats on this relationship journey.

What you have here is a start. You probably won't wrestle with your son when he's thirty, but I promise you that when he's thirty, he won't forget wrestling with you. Building a great relationship begins now, from scratch. You have the opportunity to begin building an expectation that you will "mix it up" with him at any time. Today that means physically, but in the future it will translate into working together on problems, helping each other in your lives as you grow together. Keep in mind that most of your life will be spent with your son as an adult. You both are passing through boyhood now, but it will be over very soon. Wrestle while you may.

ACTION TO **TAKE** Step into physical action with your son. Invite him down on the floor tonight for some wrestle time. If you can't do that, at least put your arm around him and say, "I love you."

CHAPTER 8

Why Won't This Stinkin' Kid Talk?

>
>
> When you finally do get your boy to speak, the process can be very frustrating. You can learn a few tricks to open up your son quickly and communicate with clarity and understanding. To miss this lesson might be to miss some powerful opportunities to connect with your son.

BOYS JUST DON'T GET IT

A while back my son Jake was going through an unusually quiet period in his life, and I was dying to know what he was thinking about. I'd sit him down and quiz him on all the big topics like baseball, newspaper routes, and friendships gone sour, that sort of stuff. I was being a paranoid dad, but I thought a little of that was allowed. Jake would always duck my questions with a bored stare, a wiggle in the chair, and a shrug. It drove me frothy at the mouth.

Once I had to ask him, "Jake, why do you hate talking to me so much? After all, I'm just trying to help." He gave me a dour look and said, "Dad, talking to you makes me itch."

"I beg your pardon," I choked.

"Yeah, Dad. Whenever you want to talk, you make me sit down, and it makes me itchy!"

"Well, why don't you answer my questions, and then I won't have to torture you anymore?" I suggested.

"*Dad,* you don't understand."

"Help me understand," I wisely tried.

"I can't think when I'm itching," he replied, beginning to squirm. Checkmate. I shut up and let him go.

LET'S SUMMARIZE THE PROBLEM

The problem here is twofold. The first fold is a tendency for your boy to talk less to you as he gets older and to clam up for strange reasons. This situation pressurizes quickly because you have a relentless need to converse with him. Parents are naturally curious (or paranoid) about what their sons are thinking, and they will turn any doorknob or pick any lock necessary to get inside.

The second fold arises from your need to ask good questions and the confusions inherent in all verbal communication. Don't make the mistake of thinking that what your boy says is what he means. Most conversations are not what they appear to be, and you make literal interpretations of spoken words at the risk of massive error! Deciphering what a boy means based on what he says is very tricky.

OPENING YOUR BOY UP

Some specific ingredients will make him clam up, and the other procedures will make him open like a faucet. Let's first look at the mechanics of a clam-up to find insights for fixing the problem.

Boys are unaware of how badly we seek to know them. Though we learned in the last chapter to relate through physical contact, what about our need to talk? As adults, we lean heavily on talking to communicate with others. Talking is something we're good at. It's practical and gets the message delivered. We are so dependent on talking that when it wheezes and sputters to a stop with our boys, we become immediately frustrated. We almost reactively begin to wonder what they're hiding.

Adults are skillful at figuring out what people are hiding. We are all good mind readers. We know from experience that people erect barriers to prevent us from knowing what they think: We all intuitively understand that people use their tongues more to hide information than to reveal it. So, we employ tricks and methods to tease out that information we suspect lies hidden in others, especially kids.

This really gets bizarre when you consider that each side—for example, an adult and an older child—knows the other is playing these hiding games. We spend a good deal of time playing this cat-and-mouse game, guessing about what is *not* being said. "What does he really mean by that?" you might wonder. "Is he really serious?" We get pretty good at guessing. We have to because hiding is the nature of people.

Boys can easily thwart every effort to get inside them. Though we know that boys need to open up to grow further in Renaissance character, getting them to do so is another matter. Boys have neither our facility with the language nor our ability to read and interpret what's hidden. The language we manage with such refinement, they stumble and bumble with. Therefore, speaking with an adult is intimidating to a boy.

The difficulties arising from this disparity can really pressurize a parent-child relationship, especially since most kids don't look like they have any trouble expressing themselves. Don't be fooled; boys are very easily confused in conversations.

For now, you must live with the truth that the best conversation possible is equal to the ability of the least conversant person. That will, in most cases, be your kid.

THE SHOOT-OUT

When your boy won't talk to you, you feel an immediate personal rejection. "You're too dumb to help me" is how you interpret his saying, "Just forget it." There are a variety of reasons your son might clam up, many having nothing to do with you. As your boy grows and changes, he naturally withdraws from the childlike naive openness of a five-year-old to a bit more selective way of interacting. He's not nearly so inclined to share with you all that's going on as he did when he was younger, and you'll have more frequent experiences of his clamming up. That's the first link in a chain of potential trouble.

The rest of the chain develops rapidly. Nobody likes feeling spurned by a child, so you move to do something. You turn down the screws, turn up the heat, cajole, laugh and pat him on the back, or prod him to get more information. Chain link #2. He doesn't answer and seems to become more stubborn (link #3). WHOOOOM! You erupt. I call this set of problems the shoot-out, and it's a classic pattern in many homes.

The prime reason driving boys to clam up is what psychologists call *demand characteristics.* Demand characteristics are the unspoken expectations and pressures boys sense in social situations that hint how they are to behave. We all are constantly bombarded with such cues, and our brains are tuned to find them, accurately interpret them, and act in response.

One Christmas, we visited the home of some friends for the first time. When we walked in the door, there was a coat tree in the foyer, a fairly obvious first clue about where to put our coats. The kids, not having ever seen a coat tree before, didn't know what to do; they had no obvious clues about what to do or where to go, so they stood quietly by. Had nobody told them what to do, they would have stood there and observed until they figured out what was appropriate, then acted accordingly.

Boys are hyperalert to these cues, and they apply riveting attention to figure out what's expected. Noticing these pressures and responding to the expectations are important to boys because they want to please adults. If a boy feels for any reason that he doesn't or can't understand what's expected of him in a situation, he'll become quiet and watch.

Not knowing this, you as a well-meaning parent turn up the pressure to pry out information. Do you see how that could happen? You ask more questions at a faster pace, hoping desperately for a response. This changes the atmosphere of the conversation. The pitch and volume of your voice shift, and your looks become more intense. None of these changes get past the ever-sharpening instincts of your son. Frustration displays itself as anger in the ears of a boy. He hasn't the slightest idea how to handle the deteriorating situation, so he does what's natural: nothing. He squirms and fidgets and tries to get away, which to your eyes looks like loathsome obstinacy. Bang! Bang! Boom! The shoot-out is under way!

It can be even more subtle. A close friend of mine was discussing the shoot-outs he was having with his son. He had tried everything imaginable to speak properly to his son, be kind and fatherly, and so on, but nothing worked. His boy would reactively clam up the instant his dad approached him about anything.

Five minutes with the boy revealed that whenever he saw his dad's face get flushed (an easily mistaken demand characteristic), he'd become scared to death. He thought it meant his dad was getting ready to blow; in reality his father was simply light complected! The boy was shutting down out of terror but drawing the wrong conclusions. The fix? I had the dad and son make a bag for the dad to wear over his head each time they wanted to chat. It worked fine because the boy didn't know when it was time to become scared.

The problem can become much more serious than this. You can, over the course of time, become frustrated and embittered, perhaps even giving up on your son. He can feel perplexed at what he sees as unmerited rejection. After a few tense interactions, the entire relationship can descend into deep muck. Nothing moves forward, communication dissolves, and a bad habit is seeded.

Let's look at how to create a win-win situation in this shoot-out and avoid habitual clam-ups.

HOW DO EXPERT COMMUNICATORS DO IT?

Earlier, I mentioned that some people are crackerjacks at relating to kids. Children have unusual trust in these special adults, and both seem to mesh effortlessly with each other. Perhaps you know adults like this, or you are fortunate enough to be one. If not, you should know that the talents they employ grow through experience and are learnable. What are these communicators doing?

1. Aggressive Listening

I taught a small group of parents that you listen best with your eyes. I suggested a riveting experiment that clearly proved the point. I had the parents practice looking deeply into the eyes of their kids. Not just casual glancing, but deeply focused, laser-like attention. "Look into the backs of their eyes. Absorb them in your gaze," I suggested.

Try it yourself! It's common for boys in this situation to ask, "What's wrong with you?" Why? For starters, they aren't used to having someone pay aggressive attention to what they are saying. Furthermore, many boys aren't familiar with having someone really try to understand what they are saying!

Unless you've been living in a cave somewhere, you've probably heard of active listening. It appeared in the early sixties as a system of psychotherapy. Active listening encouraged listeners to make good eye contact, nod their heads occasionally, and make appropriate sounds ("uh-huh," "hmmmm," "oh, my!"). That was all very commendable because for the first time people could successfully model actions of naturally gifted communicators. Best of all, the speaker felt listened to, which proved remarkably therapeutic.

An excellent communicator takes this whole idea and turns the intensity up a few clicks. He does more than listen and respond: He looks carefully at the boy and intensely focuses on not only what's said but how it's said. He offers penetrating responses to statements by thinking carefully about words and context and logic.

2. Sensitivity to Incongruencies

An incongruency is a sophisticated and unconscious double message in your speaking. Saying that you love your dog while shaking your head no. Telling your boss you can make that sale, all the while turning white, quivering, and beginning to sweat. Telling someone that you want to be near him as you snicker and back away! These are all examples of statements and behaviors that don't match or mesh with each other.

We frequently commit these incongruencies in our conversations with others. We don't do it on purpose; incongruencies are the result of normal, unchecked internal confusion that we experience and have learned to live with. The most obvious question for a listener is, "Which one do I believe, what I hear or what I see? Does he love the dog or not?"

Master communicators are crafty in observing and challenging these incongruencies with boys. Their flair is for initiating conversation without creating defensiveness. Their conversational magic allows them to hurdle the apparent conflict while making the boys feel understood and respected.

3. Active Language and Interesting Ideas

Master communicators have a good command of the language. They use active words and colorful expressions. I have little trouble getting kids to talk with me because I usually come "off the wall" with them, though I don't consider myself a comedian. This kind of interaction is easy and entertaining for boys to participate in. Perhaps you know people who are tastefully dramatic in their use of inflections and tones and cute words. If language is at all unusual, you can bet boys will notice.

Interesting ideas grab attention. If you ask boys if they have any good worm recipes, they will stop, guaranteed, and tell you their thoughts. The weirder the idea, the more likely they will be to respond to you. Expert communicators use these sorts of interesting and strange ideas to arrest the attention of listeners long enough to engage them in conversation.

4. Attracting Conversations

Using the assortment of talent listed here, these master communicators attract conversations out of boys rather than force the dialogue.

What are they doing that's so attractive? A good friend of mine is one of these charismatic, entertaining individuals who always has kids climbing on him (take note!). He can do a variety of tricks with kids, including a popular gag where he appears to lift a kid up by the hair. Although they are really holding on to his arms and hanging down, they appear to be suspended by their hair. He can then shake them around like he's King Kong! The kids line up for it! He has an almost magical ability to keep boys responding to him. You will find this universal ability among these great communicators: lighthearted physical fun followed by eager and interested dialogue.

LEARNING WHAT THE MASTERS KNOW IS LIKE EATING AN ELEPHANT

You can learn to do any of this, but can you eat an elephant? Of course, you can—one tiny bite at a time. Can you become a master communicator? Yes, one step at a time. I am going to share with you a list of specific activities you can do to build these four talents in yourself. Your instructor is very experienced and wise. Your teacher is life.

Your job? Eat and act. Eat and act! EAT AND ACT! It's not enough to read these ideas; you must have an experience with them. What are the bites you must take to become a master? You must find a few of the following techniques that suit you well and apply them daily. The targeted talents of the masters we've described will grow as your application becomes your personal habit.

NINE CLAM OPENERS

These suggestions provide a means to remove the shield of silence that slides between your boy and you. These are learnable capabilities of a Renaissance maker. Remember when eating something bigger than you, chew each bite slowly.

Clam Opener #1: Change Your Expectations

Your expectations create pressures in your life and in the lives of those around you. Without awareness, you telegraph hints to others about what you expect from them. Often your boy responds with hesitation and defensiveness, launching the classic clam-up.

Expectations are complex signaling systems necessary for a contented life. That might strike you as a strange statement, but consider that an experience cannot satisfy or disappoint you until you make an internal comparison about what you expected. You cannot, for instance, know that it's time to feel good or bad about something without first making a mental comparison against what you expected.

If your son is acting like a total jerk, and you expect that, your life will continue unchanged. If, on the other hand, you expect your son to be gracious and thoughtful, but he acts jerky, your expectations signal you that it's time to be upset. Your expectations set the dials for evaluating what's happening to you in all situations.

To apply this clam opener, write down briefly what you expect from your conversations with your boy. Start with the last talk you had with your boy. What did you expect to get out of the talk? How did you really expect your son to respond? Did he do what you thought he would do? What sort of reaction did that get from you?

You should start to see a pattern of expectations that influences all your parent-son conversations. It may also tip you to what specific expectations trigger what attitudes within the confines of your dialogues.

I was once referred to a kid who had a bad attitude and a reputation to match. I expected trouble on the first visit, and I got it. I expected him to be confused, and he was. I expected simmering anger, and I found it. All those negative expectations bothered me, so I made a conscious effort to change what I expected.

On the follow-up visit, I decided to expect a hidden urge for happiness. I found it. I made myself expect a boy very capable of laughter. I found that too. I expected to find a boy who wanted to find ways to make his life better. Shazaaam! I got that too!

For the fun of it, alter your expectations regarding talkativeness and notice what happens. Adjust the strength of your expectation if nothing else. Increase or decrease some element of expectation, and notice the change.

Clam Opener #2: Change Your Metaphor

A great friend of mine, Dan Schaefer, is a professional counselor and fellow thinker about life. Once we were both feeling particularly frazzled about the frustrations of the psychotherapy trade, and we were having a "what's it like for you" talk about changing people. He was a terrific wrestler in high school and college, and so naturally, he said, "It's like wrestling. We circle the mat a few times, slap each other around a little bit, I go for the takedown, and I try to pin 'em." No wonder, we concluded, he always felt so tired and beaten at the end of the day!

My metaphor was a chess match. Wit for wit. Move for move. Think, strategy, crinkle forehead, finger strategically positioned at the lip, splitting headache after the day! Victory? Occasionally, but usually just draws. No fun!

The token Jungian in our counseling practice was a rather cool guy whose metaphor was sitting on the bank of a river and throwing in stones at different spots. Well, that sounds pretty Jungian, and that explained why he always looked so well rested at the end of the day. Funny thing is, I tried it the next day by relaxing and throwing conversational pebbles. I didn't get a headache. Honestly, I had fun, and I felt a sudden surge of optimism about the people I had seen.

Your metaphor for your activities holds great sway over your experience. What's your metaphor for working, being married, parenting, playing, and talking with your son? There are no right or wrong answers here, just metaphors. In talking with your son, is the metaphor two friends playing happily, is it like God and Adam going over the rules, is it like trimming the rosebushes or pirouetting on the ice, or is it like charming a cobra? Think.

Clam Opener #3: Create New Atmospheres

As I've been sitting here typing, I've had the feeling of the Christmas spirit come over me. I just started thinking about how much I like the season, the weather, and the music. The music. The music. I stopped long enough to realize that in the next room, my daughter Jessie is listening to Christmas carols on a CD player. For the last ten minutes, I have been seduced by the music she's playing, and I thought I was being nostalgic on my own!

There are infinite varieties of emotional atmospheres around us at all times. We don't notice them because we are in them. Yet they exert strong control over what we feel and how we act. The most important thing to remember, however, is that these atmospheres can become part of specific, actual locations. You walk into the kitchen and feel like eating; you walk into your bedroom and feel like lying down; you walk into your son's bedroom and feel like leaving!

You must assume responsibility for an effective talking atmosphere. When difficulty emerges in talking with your son, feel absolutely free to change the venue. Go for a walk. Take a drive. Change shirts. Chew gum. Do anything! Assume responsibility for changing the atmosphere of pressure and stagnation to something different.

Clam Opener #4: Find Your Boy's Hot Buttons

Is there a topic that really turns you on? Cars? Sports? Money? Well, your boy has a favorite topic too. All the boys in our neighborhood are into baseball cards, Rollerblades, Play Station 2, and incendiary devices. These items pepper their conversations.

Everybody is psychologically orbiting around things of greatest personal interest. Each person's orbit has distinct features, hot buttons, which you can notice if you observe a little. Your boy's hot buttons may not be of great interest to you, but let me encourage you about something. You needn't like *his* interests to use them as a fulcrum upon which to lever conversations. You just need to spend twenty minutes to familiarize yourself with the things he finds important and interesting. Find twenty minutes and make a sound investment in your future.

If you don't know your son's hot buttons, ask him. You might be surprised to find that what you thought he liked, he doesn't much care for. A mother I know recently discovered that her son, a rabid baseball card fanatic, wasn't really that interested in cards; he just loved to go to the store to spend money! Hot buttons are not always what they appear to be!

Clam Opener #5: Talk Specifically About Interesting Things

For boys (and some of us), it's easier to talk about a chair than it is to talk about happiness. You can connect with football much easier than you can connect with self-control. Notice the concrete, touchable characteristic of some things, and the abstract, misty quality of others?

Boys don't get the misty stuff. To have good talks, you must have skill at speaking in concrete terms about concrete topics. Adults get wrapped up in abstractions, so you need to make a pointed effort to keep your boy talks on solid and touchable topics.

Make yourself alert for one new and interesting topic each day. Many of these topics are floating around. Sources could be the newspaper (talk about fires, politics, civil wars in other countries, etc.), strange job experiences, or other people's weird stories! Train your ears to listen for these oddities.

I try to make it a point to read encyclopedias as much as possible. Why, the other day, for no reason other than to test my theory, I grabbed the V volume and happened upon Vikings, where I read the most amazing facts.

My kids and I spent the whole dinnertime that night talking about Vikings. They were spellbound. It took perhaps sixty seconds to read over the information so I could repeat it in a conversational fashion. Find topics like this, and exert a little effort to commit them to memory for your boy's sake. The more concrete and simple, the better.

Clam Opener #6: Use Odd Words and Strange Language

Boys like odd-sounding words and non sequiturs. Always be on the hear-out for words that strike you as having pizzazz or sparkle or flair. The words might come as popular phrases or occur in stories you read. Ask your son to find out what's currently hot.

Or try an easy non sequitur. A non sequitur is a statement that does not follow from the previous comment or thought. It's a word or comment out of sequence. The simplest non sequiturs are out words of order. I mean, words out of order. They are irritating to the listener (especially your boy) and beg to be corrected. If you skip words, rearrange them, or completely blister a pronunciation, all hearers, boys especially, have an urge to fix the mistake.

Try these: "Please clarify you what mean," or "Is there any help way I can you now?" or maybe "It's time for bed to you out of get."

Correcting a non sequitur is a terrific clam opener because it forces your boy to listen to you and respond to you. Whenever you sense a boy coming toward you, the control of the interaction is yours. That moment of curiosity is the first link in a new chain moving him from clamhood to chatterbox.

Clam Opener #7: Look for Unguarded Moments

If you choose to be a nimble communicator, become alert to moments when your son is suddenly talkative. The openings have a cycle when, for whatever reason, your boy is in a talkative mood. This cycle is unusually pronounced in boys older than age eight, but it is present in all boys. You should be capable of responding to the fleeting moods by dropping everything and jumping into the fray.

The worst time to look for these is when he's shelled up. As a family therapist, I saw countless occasions when parents chose the quiet moments to machine-gun their son with tirades about lack of respect and never talking. I've experienced the common parental impulse to pry him open by any available means, but that creates agony for everyone and prolongs the shoot-out.

I've finally learned that when I'm getting the runaround from some uncooperative kid, it's time to go for a walk. No pressure. No time concerns. Just walk and talk.

Boys will open up when they are tired, relaxed, excited, or happy about something unusually joyous. Bedtimes, mealtimes, drive times, and after-school times are all potential moments.

Clam Opener #8: "We Have Ways to Make You Talk"

I've met parents who would've been outstanding Nazi interrogators. They seem to understand how to scare the wits out of kids. Don't intimidate your son on purpose. He doesn't like it, and neither should you. Sometimes the most effective thing you can do to pierce the shield of silence is to back off.

No matter how good of a parent you are, you can always learn to use a little more tact. Treat your son like the magnificent creature he is. Don't scold yourself if you flunk the "finesse with boys" test, but don't let yourself off the hook, either. Make yourself patient with people, make yourself kind to others when you would prefer to scream, keep your cool when others are losing theirs, and be the calming source of stability when wars rage around you.

People of poise set the standards for us all. People of poison do not.

ACTION TO TAKE

Class is over. It's time to get to work. Select two or three clam openers, and apply them today. You shouldn't wait till an emergency arises to get proficient with them, and a little focused practice would be of marvelous benefit. Enjoy!

CHAPTER 9

That's a Great Question!

 There is unmistakable wisdom and strength in asking good questions. Here are some tips for using these simple tools like a surgeon.

THE ART OF THE QUESTION

Questions are versatile inventions of humankind. The ancients used questions for everything. They thought asking questions was an art form, and they used them for teaching, inquiring, and solving problems. Aristotle is the guy who first used the *peripatetic method.* This is where we've gotten the image of the bearded, robed teacher with leaves in his hair, strolling around with adoring students in tow, posing wise questions. The student thoughtfully responds, to which the master poses further questions. Questions, questions, questions. That was the way thinking was taught and education conducted for many years.

Now, let me tell you about the *very pathetic method* I see many parents using. Most parents don't ask questions; they opt instead to lecture or harangue their sons. Boys need to be asked questions. Good questions prompt thinking, pose new possibilities, and promote all aspects of mental development:

"What do you want to be?"

"Would you ever rob a store?"

"Can you imagine building a machine that could . . . ?"

"What am I hiding in my hand?"

Well-formed, clear questions teach, illuminate ideas, encourage ordered thinking, and reward you with clear answers. Master the art of the question, and you master a source of great power.

Questions fall into two broad categories: (1) clarifying what was said, and (2) eliciting information or responses from others.

1. Questions That Clarify

You should *never* believe that what you heard your son say is exactly what he meant. It's impossible for him to utter exactly what he means, let alone for you to understand it. Why? It's a bit unorthodox to discuss this, but there are natural forces at work to derail your best efforts to communicate clearly. At best, what's spoken is only a rough representation of what your boy means and should be treated as such. What are these forces, and what are they doing messing around with you?

What If a Monkey Could Type? I once heard a provocative illustration about the nature of language. If a monkey were able to sit in front of a typewriter and type English sentences, you would not be able to read what he wrote. His little monkey brain operates differently from the human brain. The products of his thinking, though typed in a language we could read, would be unintelligible because of the alignment and presentation of ideas.

Some of our problems in understanding boys are similar to this situation. No, I don't think your son is a monkey, but you'll remember the differences between boy and adult thinking. You know the specifics of what you can expect for normal BoyThink. Even under optimal conditions, a boy isn't willing to chitchat for very long. He has trees to climb, bikes to ride, girls to run away from, and so on. You, by comparison, aren't that interesting, and you must remember your place in his universe.

The Outlaws of Conversation. Our minds are like fingerprints; no two are exactly alike. Inside your mind is an incalculable variety of ideas and words, feelings and memories that are uniquely you. When you speak, you quickly sort through these experiences and funnel them down into a few short utterances called words. The words are not the exact copy of all that is going on in your mind, just a summed-up, condensed code used to represent all your unique thinking. The short, coded utterances are then sprayed through this tiny little hole in your face (called a mouth) and outward on a perilous journey to other people's ears.

In the ears of the hearer hide the outlaws. The three outlaws of communication are *generalization, deletion,* and *distortion.* They're more or less normal brain processes that succeed in creating constant havoc in communication.

Have you ever been unable to say exactly what you felt or thought? We choose words that when strung together get close to what we really want to communicate. Linguists call this process *generalization.*

Generalization works the reverse in the mind of the listener. If you say to me, "The bird is chewing bubble gum," understanding what you mean requires that I create a picture in my mind that is generally what I think you are referring to. My picture will not and cannot be perfectly like what you mean.

The real damage done by generalization is that it prevents perfectly clear communication; it washes out precision. Perfect communication between you and your son (you know exactly what he means, and vice versa) is only a dim possibility.

Next is the problem of *deletion.* Read the following phrase; then on the line underneath, write the phrase out.

Paris

in the

the spring.

Nine out of ten people write what they see: "Paris in the spring." However, if you read carefully, you will read something different. The phrase says, "Paris in the *the* spring." But you deleted some crucial information automatically without the slightest awareness. That is normal, and it goes on all the time.

I tape-record conversations whenever possible. I'm constantly amazed on the replay to hear things I never heard the first time around.

Deletion is a commonly disruptive occurrence between a parent and a child by which vital information gets ignored. It is also the root of terrific misunderstanding and a breakdown in confidence in each other. As a parent, you don't know which ideas and words are deleted and which ones your son notices. Information not registered is information lost forever. It doesn't matter what you say; if your words get deleted by the hearer (and many of them are), the effect is as if you never said them!

Distortion is the third outlaw. No doubt you have had the experience of listening to someone speak to you in perfectly normal language, but you had absolutely no idea what the person was talking about. The early seconds of such encounters are filled with your valiant attempts to decipher what is being said. You use your mind to bend and twist the information to create some meaning—any meaning—that makes sense to you!

This is a stark example of a subtle process called distortion, which goes on constantly inside our heads. We distort what we hear to fit what we know so that words make sense to us. This is a completely automatic process that helps us understand communication, at the expense of hearing exactly what is said. And we all do it: Our boys even need to distort what we say for it to make sense to them! Accurate communication is stolen at yet another turn.

You should probably sit down! All of this is as amazing as it is common. The implications are staggering for those who were rolling merrily along thinking they were great communicators. The good news is that knowing about them allows you to counteract their efforts.

How do we foil these three outlaws? By using clarifying questions. Clarifying questions come in three forms: rephrasing, if-then questions, and synonyms. Rephrasing is restating what you thought you heard and asking if that is what he meant. You might think you sound like Captain Peg Leg's parrot, repeating all the time, but the effect allows you to get highly accurate clarifications from your boy.

For example, if your son says, "I'm really tired of eating pizza every night for dinner," you would rephrase it by saying, "Oh, so eating pizza, makes you sleepy?"

"No, no, no, I'm sick of pizza!"

"Oh, so pizza makes you get nauseated?"

"No, no, no! I want meat and potatoes, Mom!"

"You want a meat-and-potatoes mom. What kid of strange kid are you?"

This silly example makes the point. Take the words your son has spoken, rework them into a new sentence that represents what you think he means, and say it back to him. Ask if that is what he means. Whatever he tells you, rephrase it and move forward. The rule of thumb is that the very closest you can get is rough understanding. If you adopt this rule, you will be forever careful how you handle what's said and pursue deeper explorations and clarifications.

If-then questions clarify the meaning someone is trying to convey by creating logical inferences. If your son says, "I'm thirsty" as he looks in the refrigerator, you might respond by saying, "If you're thirsty, then why are you looking in the refrigerator?" His clarification might be something like, "I'm thirsty for a soft drink."

When your son says, "I want to go swimming," you might logically suggest, "If you want to go swimming, then you must be hot." Who knows how he might respond? He might say, "No, my friends are going," or "No, I just want to get out of the house for a while." His reply adds to the cause of increasing clarity. These questions focus and clarify the meaning *behind* what's said. Be creative with this, and try it out in varying circumstances.

Requesting synonyms can be very helpful, too. You ask your son to clarify his point by using a different example:

- "Would you please say that another way?"

- "Could you give me an example of what you mean?"

- "Could you act out or show me what you mean?"

These are all requests to show in another way (a synonymous action) what he's talking about. It is a very penetrating way to translate what your boy is trying to express.

Have you ever received the "oh, just forget it" treatment from your son? It comes from the impatience and disgust he feels with your inability to comprehend what he is saying. He thinks it's easy! Be patient. Encourage him to try a different way to say the same thing.

2. Questions That Elicit Information

Brilliant conversationalists will tell you they aren't that brilliant. They understand that people love to talk about themselves, so they ask their listeners lots of questions. The listeners think these people are brilliant! Such brilliant conversationalists have mastered the art form of asking questions for information and responses. Whatever brilliance they possess is in the intuitive realization that questions have power to make things happen. Questions used properly can persuade, gather information, plant ideas, clear up thinking, motivate, solve problems, overcome objections, gain cooperation, take the bite out of criticism, or defuse explosive situations.

Inquiry-type questions are typically open or closed. Closed questions elicit yes or no responses:

- "Are you sick?"
- "Do you want to go to the movies?"
- "Would you give me a million dollars?"

They are great for gathering simple and quick information, but they usually don't reveal substantial information. When possible, closed questions need to be changed to open questions.

Open questions allow elaborate answers. Dorothy Leeds in her excellent book *Smart Questions* reveals that open questions are created with three critical openings: "What . . . ?" "How . . . ?" and "Could . . . ?" Any question you could possibly ask can be opened with one of these three leadoffs. Their elegance is that they encourage responses in the most pressure- free way. When asked questions of this sort, a boy is practically led by the hand to find new answers and elaborate on previously stated positions.

I want you to commit this list of questions to memory. They will be very useful in drawing information out of your son:

- "What can I do to help?"
- "What has to be done?"
- "Could you explain a little more?"
- "How does that make you feel?"
- "Could you tell me what your reason is for asking?"
- "What needs to change?"
- "What are you trying to accomplish?"
- "How can I talk to you so you will want to talk to me?"
- "What do you want?"

- "What's happening now?"

- "What stops you from getting what you want?"

- "What do you need to reach your goal?"

- "How will you know if you're moving toward your goal?"

Any question you want to ask can be turned into a creative *what-how-could* question. Questions like these lead to good, useful answers. They work almost like magic, so apply them liberally and creatively. You can get any information you want if you pose the question properly. A little experimentation is all you need to get a taste of real success. You can't make any mistakes, so try.

I once had to convince a very physically strong child not to let weaker bullies pound on him. The poor child was getting treated mercilessly by other boys, and there was no physical, pecking-order-type reason for it. Notice in the following exchange the occasional sprinkling of open questions to encourage the boy's elaboration:

"What does blood from busted teeth taste like?"

"Yuck," he said.

"Are you enjoying this kind of treatment?"

"No," he murmured.

"Can I help you find a new solution?"

"Yes," he whispered.

"What will that solution look like?"

"It will look like people will treat me nice," he said.

"Do you know anyone treated nice in school?" I asked.

"Why did you avoid asking *why* questions?" you might ask. No, ask like this: "What was your purpose in avoiding *why* questions?"

Why Questions Are Dead Ends. Asking *why* will usually get a conversation stuck. It's also a very demanding question that will invariably create defensiveness and confusion:

- "Why are you looking at me like that?"

- "Why did you say that?"

- "Why do you let those kids beat up on you?"

Do you sense the pressure, the urgency? *Why* questions are demanding on everyone, and boys will typically respond to that pressure by freezing.

What-how-could questions suggest new ways to think. They pose inquiry in a form that can be answered. They retrieve *why* information in a much more sensible form.

Why questions usually pop up during situations of duress: "Why did you do that?" or "Why do you always ignore me?" These quickly put the listeners on the defensive. They do nothing to gain information, and they usually serve the limited purpose of letting your son know you are mad or disappointed. These are the moments to ask different questions.

Transform your *why* questions, and avoid the stress of a grinding halt in communication. *Why* questions can be reframed in the *what-how-could* form and made ten times more effective. Be creative.

ACTION TO TAKE

I've covered many ideas. They are all fabulous, but you can't know that just by reading. You must have an experience with an idea for it to become real. Try this: For thirty minutes, force yourself to talk with your son in questions. No comments are allowed. Whenever he says anything, reply with a question. If you want to tell him something, make the statement in the form of a question. You will find that the application of this exercise will expand your knowledge of how asking questions can broadly affect a boy's talking. One idea applied is better than one thousand learned.

CHAPTER 10

Fueling the Idea Machine

A Renaissance man is a combination of interlocking pieces. One of the fundamental pieces is the imaginative talent inside every boy's brain. Develop it, and give him a creative life. Ignore it, and you might not ever recover the missed opportunity.

THE QUINTESSENTIAL BOY

"Zachary, how many pieces of gum do you have in your mouth?"

"Uuugmmmmphuhu," he replied, holding up two fingers.

I took the golf-ball-sized glob of gum out of his mouth to hear him right. "How many?" I asked.

"Two, Dad. One, two, six, thirteen, ten, two!" he pleaded.

When I hear that tone, I know something's up. "Zachary! What kinda way is that to count?" I asked.

"Dad, it's a new way to count I made up called expansion."

What represents a boy better than unbridled curiosity, imagination, and creativity? His little head bursts with energy to explore the world and frolic in the playground of the mind. Innocent playfulness is the immature expression of vast mental resources. Unfortunately, the natural capability he inherits at conception is stripped like bark off a tree as he marches toward adulthood. It's tragic—and avoidable.

Maturity needn't chase away what God has so generously endowed.

Curiosity, imagination, and creativity are individual talents, each making its contribution to the sparkle and freshness we seek in life. Can we raise our boys to fully express these gifts as they get older and make these gifts remain pliant and useful into the adult years?

Of course we can. Following the Renaissance road means finding a way. A boy's brains are tough and capable of much more than you could ever ask. Help him develop overwhelming capability that will last a lifetime.

This Is Only a Test

This exercise will help you learn something. James L. Adams in his fascinating book *Conceptual Blockbusting* takes readers through a vivid exercise in imagination called *breathing*. Read each sentence, and stop at the slash to imagine. Don't move on to the next until you've done a good job. Do this with your son. See who is better.

Let us imagine we have a goldfish in front of us. / Have the fish swim around./ Have the fish swim into your mouth./ Take a deep breath and have the fish go down into your lungs, into your chest./ Have the fish swim around in there./ Let out your breath and let the fish swim out into the room again./ Now breathe in a lot of tiny goldfish./ Have them swim around in your chest./ Breathe them all out again./ Let's see what kinds of things you can breathe in and out of your chest./ Breathe in a lot of rose petals./ Breathe them out again./ Breathe in a lot of water./ Have it gurgling in your chest./ Breathe it out again./ Breathe in a lot of dry leaves./ Have them blowing around in your chest./ Breathe them out again./ Breathe in a lot of raindrops./ Have them pattering in your chest./ Breathe them out again./ Breathe in a lot of sand./ Have it blowing around in your chest./ Breathe it out again./ Breathe in a lot of firecrackers./ Have them popping in your chest./ Breathe out the smoke and the bits of them that are left./ Breathe in a lot of little lions./ Have them all roaring in your chest./ Breathe them out again./ Breathe in some fire. / Have it burning and crackling in your chest./ Breathe it out again./ Breathe in some logs of wood./ Set fire to them in your chest./ Have them roaring as they burn up./ Breathe out the smoke and the ashes./ How is that?/ Be a stone./ Don't breathe./ How do you like that?/ Be a boy (girl)./ Breathe the air of this room, in and out./ How do you like that?

If you do this with your son, you might find that he gets antsy and unfocused very quickly. His natural creative juices bubble quickly to the surface if given a chance. That's all right; you should want to keep it that way. His potential in life will be determined by how well he maintains and disciplines that curiosity, how he applies imagination, and what he creates along the road.

SOLID LINES AND DOTTED LINES

When architects create blueprints for a new building, they draw in solid lines to represent where walls are to be built, and they use dotted lines to represent where future expansions can go. Your boy's Architect has done the same with him. How good can he get? What's his potential? Where are his dotted lines? Curiosity, imagination, and creativity are the forces that will help move his solid lines (where he is at birth) to the dotted lines (the upper levels of his personal excellence). Develop these three pieces, and the dotted lines move outward into areas of greater potential. Restrict these three, and the dotted lines come rushing backward, strangling potential.

These three talents must grow and intertwine. Curiosity is innate and needs to be fed. Imagination needs inspiration and room to explode. Creativity needs points of focus and outlets for expression.

They are all different and all critical. Building a Renaissance man requires focusing these three together like a laser beam. Now is the time for you to increase the amplitude of your efforts.

FEEDING CURIOSITY

Let's suppose for a moment that I were to give you a small laptop computer that learned all by itself and collected data and information all on its own. Though it would be slow at first, ask some dumb questions and make simple mistakes, it would learn. Later, it would pick up speed and really fly, eventually knowing too much for its own good! There is only one thing you must, absolutely must, give it: experience. Give it experience, and it does the rest.

This little computer would be the most mind-blowing piece of equipment ever made. Nothing ever created could come close to the performance spec. Well, surprise! You've got one of these computers at home now, and he has arms and legs! By design, he's motivated to take the measure of the world and figure out the best path of growth. The only sustenance you need to provide is experience. He can do all the rest.

Think of curiosity as having a life of its own inside your boy. It's very active, and your son can't control it well. I suspect as boy raisers we look upon a quality such as curiosity as "being" our boys rather than a quality that our sons possess. Your son isn't curious; he has curiosity.

You don't feed your son; you feed his curiosity. How do you feed it? First, you have to find it. Get your son. I want you to see something.

Tell him he has eleven fingers, and you can prove it. Coax him a little bit to wonder how in the world you can prove that, and watch the look of curiosity that consumes him. It is very noticeable once you learn to recognize it. He will get still, his eyes will become focused and intense, and you will notice a distinct sparkle. That's the look of curiosity.

Now, show him he has eleven fingers. Take one hand, and count the fingers 1, 2, 3, 4, 5. Then with the other hand, count the fingers backward, 10, 9, 8, 7, 6. Then do the obvious addition: 5 + 6 = 11.

He may not be perfectly astounded, so take another step to get a good look at the sight of curiosity. Tell him to tell his buddies that they have eleven fingers and he can prove it! Watch him carefully. You will see curiosity clearly.

Pay attention to the following public service announcement: Curiosity may present itself to you as an irritant, causing you to be blinded to its presence. It can disguise itself in your son and look like thoughtless actions, obsessiveness, and even downright stupidity. You might even think your boy is mentally troubled. These reasons explain why childhood curiosity is so often foolishly squashed.

I don't think you should let your son's curiosity run totally rampant, for that could be dangerous. But it's equally dangerous to pulverize it for the sake of making your life easier. A little discomfort isn't going to hurt you, so let your son's curiosity have a little more leash than it's had in the past.

IMAGINATION: THE QUIET INTERNAL RIOT

If you could secretly peer into others' minds during the day and see what they were thinking, you would swear they were crazy. It's a bizarre tangle of strange thoughts, secret wishes, arguments, lies, and screams. And what do most of us look like on the outside? Smooth and unruffled, controlled and serene! An amazing contrast, don't you think?

Our brains epitomize reckless imagination and uncontrolled curiosity. The lightbulbs unconsciously ping on with ideas and schemes. Fantasies launch dreams; dreams feed desires. It's completely automatic madness.

We keep a tight lid on the whole machine, though, so nobody knows what's occurring. And sometimes we control ourselves so much that we overcontrol, practically shutting off the idea maker!

The prime difference between boys and adults is that boys are less disciplined in controlling the imagination. Imagination, to run fast and well, needs a track upon which to concentrate its energy. It must be harnessed and focused. For a boy to have a fully functioning imagination, there are two requirements. First, he must be disciplined enough to control his thought processes, and second, he must have a simultaneous ability to let his imagination run wild.

Imagination without control creates problems. Boys with unruly imaginations usually have unruly energies. Unbridled energies can be very disruptive to the boys and their surroundings. Uncontrolled imagination is not natural. Kids learn to suppress themselves as they mature, and if not coached differently, they will be unable to maintain the imaginative savvy of a brightly thinking child into adulthood. Only disciplined practice will help imagination remain alive as boys grow older.

How Can You Build a Fast Track for Your Boy's Imagination?

You want to let your boy's imagination run as far to the dotted lines as possible. Some games can provide the track upon which it can run. I have used the following games and variations on them with thousands of kids over the years, and they produce a broader imagination. They form discipline by requiring simple structure and simple rules.

Free Association

This is as close to wild, unobstructed imagination as you will find in this group. (This game borrows directly from the technique that Freud used to search the minds of his patients, but where Freud was looking for meaning, we are trying only to build imagination.)

List short topics that interest your boy. Break the topics down into single words—for example, *Corvette, space shuttle, chocolate, darts, Totally Hair Barbie*—and play the game. You say the word, and he must respond with the first word or thought that comes into his head. Make this game go very fast. Don't play it for longer than sixty seconds or you'll bore him. A good rule: Always stop when your son wants you to keep going. The whole experience stays fresh that way.

Brain Twisters

Always be on the lookout for these. Many books and children's magazines have brain twisters that are perceptual tricks or odd thoughts or experiments. If you keep the presentation of these twisters simple, your boy will love them. They work by far the best if they are biology-chemistry-physics-type experiments, for they mesh well with things that spark imagination in a young boy.

I'll give you one to try immediately. It's called a Moebius Strip. It was discovered over two hundred years ago, and it has some very peculiar properties. Here is how you make one: Take a two-by-twelve-inch strip of paper, and make a loop. Before you tape the ends together, give one end a half-twist. You've just created an amazing loop; it has only one side. Prove this by taking a pencil and drawing a line down the middle of the strip completely around the loop.

That's not all. If you use scissors to cut along the line, it doesn't separate into two loops; it becomes one regular loop twice as long! If you use your imagination, you can guess what cutting it into thirds will do.

Turn-Taking Stories

You can do this with two or more people. You might think of this as progressive fiction. Sit comfortably. You, as the promoter of imagination, start by taking thirty seconds and making up the introduction to a story. The next person, be it the kid on your right or left, takes the next thirty to sixty seconds to add an imaginative section to the story, making up a continuation of your story. Person number three picks up the trail from number two as the story grows in a completely unpredictable fashion. You're finished when the circle finishes and you've added the perfect ending to the serpentine story line.

Planned Attack

Remember the game of capture the flag? Great heart-thumping, bone-smashing fun! The thrill of the hunt and planning attack maneuvers and all that great stuff! This game is a far simpler version that can be played by you the members of your family.

The point of this game is to create a map. Select something you want to attack: fire hydrants, cats, grannies, whatever. Get down on the ground, and draw a map of your attack plan with your finger, chalk, or a stick. Encourage your boy to draw in relevant obstacles, means of hiding routes of movement, and ways to move to make a successful attack. Talk about imagination! Your boy's thoughts will burst open; so don't plan on leaving soon.

Witty Ditties

Albert Ellis, a prolific and provocative psychotherapist, recommends the use of witty ditties to launch his patients into a better state of mental health. Witty ditties are funny rhymes, poems, limericks, and songs poking fun at things troubling the patient. Clinical patients typically find it hard to joke about serious matters, so the introduction of taboo-busting rhymes allows a fresh perspective on stagnant problems. Remember rule challenges?

Rhyme anything and everything you can think of. No need to have a special time and place for these, but be ever mindful and on the lookout for opportunities. They might pop into your head anytime: "Hey, dude, how's the attitude? You look a little crude. This will help your mood; eat a little bit of food." Load your imaginative cannons to be an impromptu poet, and encourage your boy to do likewise.

Jokes

I was never a good joke teller. But I found that I could read them with the same effect! Jokes and riddles are excellent sources of double meanings, wordplays, and rhythms in humor. Most kids' magazines are sources of jokes. Read them as often as possible, and of course, make up jokes at will. Don't tell me you can't just because you never have. I know it might be embarrassing, but remember this: Why didn't the skeleton cross the road? No guts!

Adventures

The word *adventure* means something special to a boy. It sounds exotic, interesting, and fun. You needn't be Indiana Jones to do this. An adventure is anything out of the ordinary that you call an adventure. I like to tell my kids that we are going on a drive to get totally lost. I start to whistle the theme to *Raiders of the Lost Ark,* and their eyes bulge! They beg to go home! Do anything with your boy, preface it as an adventure, and suddenly it's magical.

However, do your best to make the adventure a slightly novel experience. Use your imagination. Find a three-story building and tell your son that you are going to climb it on the outside! He'll look at you, coyly smile, then frown. You don't have to climb it to make it adventurous. Walk up to it, look up its walls, and try to get a toehold. Your boy will think you're nuts, and he'll soon figure out that it can't be done (at least by you). But at least you thought about it and tried.

Consider John Goddard. As a teenager, John decided that he was going to live a special life, so he sat down and wrote a list. He called it "My Life List," consisting of 127 things he wanted to do before he died. It defined for him the adventurous life: climbing Mount Everest, milking a poisonous snake, sky diving, becoming an Eagle Scout, visiting the North and South Poles, and so on. To date, he has completed 108 of the 127!

The Yiddish term for brazenness and gall is *chutzpah* (hoot-spa). I suppose if any word summarizes my approach with boys, it's this one. You've seen people with it; obnoxious and gutsy, yet, secretly you wish for a little taste of it! A small dose of chutzpah will put a large charge of action into every adventure. Become outlandish and ask people if you can do things; you'll be amazed at what people let you do! Ask to tour a police station; ask the butcher if he has a cow tongue you can have for dinner; go to the top floor of an office building; go to a local airport and ask to sit in the cockpit of a jet. Preface your request by saying, "My son has never done this. May we?" Be gutsy, and take your son on a true adventure.

What-Ifs

You can use conversational what-ifs frequently. Their purpose is to prompt thinking and imagination in a gentle, thoughtful way: "What if that letter carrier could deliver mail on a surfboard?" and similar queries. You can use your imagination and think these up spontaneously as you go. As I mentioned earlier, our brains are well equipped to dream up strange and catchy what-ifs. Fire them out at your boy, and let him respond to them. Nine out of ten times he will respond with equally imaginative constructions! Welcome them.

Wing It!

When I was a kid, I used to watch the then-popular comedian Jonathan Winters do a segment of his television show called "Wing it!" This segment was a lot like the current hit show *Whose Line Is It Anyway?* wherein someone is pitched an idea or a prop and asked to make something funny with it on the spot. It sounds hard, but with some practice you can learn to do the funniest things with just the simplest household things or the simplest idea. You can take a broom and fly like a witch, make a wig for your head, brush your teeth, play it like a guitar, etc. It's just imagination used in a fun way.

When my kids were small, I used to hand them objects with the request to wing it. After your boy warms and adjusts to the whole weird idea, he will be very good. You will even find him doing it spontaneously, which is the sure sign that something you've initiated has caught on.

Projectives

Projective tests are psychological means of measuring people based on their responses to ambiguous pictures and figures. For example, the fascinating Children's Apperception Test shows drawings of animals in human repose, and it asks children to make up a story about what is going on in the drawings. The variations in response are imaginative and telling!

Pick out any picture in your house, and try this with your son. Ask him to make up a story, telling you what each person is thinking, what will happen next, how the story ends, and so on. You can draw a picture with stick figures and do the same questioning if you like. I've done a completely original variation of this with scribbles.

My daughter Jessica was going to learn how to write in cursive, and she was nervous about not being able to learn the lettering. I told her that she already knew how to write in cursive, but nobody had ever shown her. She disagreed with me and made me prove it.

This is what I did: I asked her to scribble all over the piece of paper. Then I took a marker and went around the page highlighting all the cursive letters I could find in the jumble of lines (you can easily find all the letters from A to Z). I was lucky enough to find a string of the letters *JES* and told her that not only could she write in cursive, but she could spell her name!

We continued to search the page, finding short words, faces, and symbols. Since she scribbled it, I made her tell me the story behind all the faces, which she was happy to do. A perfect projective pulls out information that you imagine you see.

Faces

I included making faces here because I think it's important to develop expressive facial muscles. Our faces are prime nonverbal communication channels, and your boy should be good at using his. Make faces, copy faces that you see, trade goofy looks, impersonate famous people, do impressions, and generally play games with your looks.

Personalities

Boys try on for size countless identities. They think an identity is something you choose rather than the way you are. They usually don't figure that out till many choices and years later.

Taking on another a personality is nothing more than using your imagination to act like someone else would act. Maybe you want to act like Gilligan, Marco Polo, or Batman. Encourage your son to have the playfulness and imagination to wear these personas like pajamas. Refer to him as the person he is wearing. Have some fun with this. Feel free to pick one and play the role yourself. It's a fun stretch of your imagination.

CREATIVITY: HARDWARE IN NEED OF A SKILLED USER

In most schemes for developing creativity, the three processes (curiosity, imagination, and creativity) get condensed together. All the techniques for enhancing them are applied to the whole glob rather than individually. I've separated them here because of the terrific value in learning to do each separately.

We've learned about the first two, so how does creativity fit? Creativity is intentionally focused curiosity and imagination for a solution to a specific problem or objective. If there is no focus or no point, there's no creativity—just aimless curiosity and vain imagination. True creativity is like an engine fueled by curiosity and imagination to get something done.

I once counseled a young boy who had a football fetish. He had something like twenty footballs in his room, all flat and ruined. I found him to be a nice kid of average intelligence—with no real obsession with pigskins. His problem was that his parents bought him cheap footballs that soon lost their air, so they had to keep buying new ones if their son was to keep playing.

After I'd gotten all the details, I asked the boy if he was ever curious about why footballs lost air. He told me that though he'd wondered about it a little, he never really investigated why it happened. So I gave him the homework assignment of dissecting one of his old, useless footballs to find out why it had lost its air.

A week later, my little friend returned, proudly displaying the black rubber bladder of a disemboweled football. He told me with great excitement that he had found a hole in the bladder. "Do you think you can fix it?" I asked. After some blank looks, his face lit up as he said, "I could put a bandage on it!" A week later he came back with his semi-soft, mangled-looking football still holding air.

Now I ask you, what happened? This little guy never looked at his footballs with a determination to fix them. He never positioned himself to create a solution. His most creative solution to the problem had been, "Mom, I need a new ball." He had the hardware for creating (his brain) but not the slightest idea how to use it.

Creativity is a learned talent. Begin to think of it as a practical, applicable skill to develop in your son. Like most of the other traits of Renaissance caliber, you are the catalyst that generates the growth spurt. Let's talk about how you can do that.

WHOSE NEURONS GET SIZZLED?

You cannot be creative for your son, just as you cannot be curious or imaginative for him. You can remind him of these options, and you can urge him to open up and use them, but the neurons that sizzle need to be his. That happens when you prime the pump and get out of the way.

Creative application of brainpower takes some practice, and it needs to become a habit over time. Be patient. You'll find yourself priming your boy's creative pump, seeing it work for a while, then helplessly watching it chug to a stop. That is common. Prime it again and keep going. Prime it till he takes over for himself.

A group of kids in our neighborhood were going to collectively build a project for an invention convention at the local school. They came to me for advice on building a perpetual-motion machine. I suggested that they try something using gravity. After plinking around in vain for an hour, they were out of ideas. They came back, and I suggested static electricity. They tried and tried but came up with no ideas. "How about something with a siphon?" I suggested. No go. They couldn't make a siphon that would keep running without outside help.

"How about something with magnets?" I offered. Magnets? MAGNETS! Yes! They were off and running! They came back later with an idea for a perpetual-motion machine that was very clever. Prime the little pumps till they run, and you will never be able to shut them off.

In a moment, we will consider different creative outlets you can use for practice. Creativity within any of these outlets is mathematically infinite. Your son might have thought up all the solutions he thinks he can create when many more are possible. Due to your experience and wisdom, you will see other solutions to challenges, but bite your tongue. He needs to find them out for himself. Don't spoon-feed him, though it might be easier and faster. Encourage him. Slowly teach him to build a refined ability of thinking and creating on his own.

How Do You Build Creativity?

I suggest that you build outputs for visual and musical creativity and for problem-solving creativity. Let's look at each.

Building Visual and Musical Creativity Outputs

Let me preface this section by telling you that I am not talking about creating career painters, sculptors, or musicians. I am talking about building outputs for the mental creativity undergirding these talents. Your son may not have the talent to be a Picasso or a Prokofiev, but that doesn't mean to forget the creating and composing!

The outlets for this type of creative energy are things to draw on and things to play on. Using these outlets for creative intentions comes with familiarity and encouragement. You need to make your boy aware of instruments, either by teaching him to whistle or by buying him a Steinway. A boy needs to know about all the outlets available, and he needs to be shown how they work.

A boy doesn't know that paints make great images on paper or that clay can be formed into cool figurines. He must be told. If you want him to understand the creative challenge in composing a tune or sculpting a figure, it's your job to show him the output choices. The more outputs, the better.

Then comes the fun part. Encourage a creation by doing it with him. Roll up your sleeves and touch the clay; get some paint on your fingers. Act excited, even if it doesn't thrill you. Prompt and guide and start something specific, then get out of the way! I've noticed that once you get kids going, you create an avalanche.

Make Up Songs. Compose a song on the spot using your voices, no instruments. Anybody can do that. If you've never done it, it's because you're afraid it will be no good. Forget no good!

What's to lose? It might be easiest to start by taking a popular song and adding your own words. Make up any string of words, even total nonsense if you like. The point is to stretch the vocal cords and get your mind in gear. Let your hair down, and have some fun. If you can add original melodies, so much the better.

We've had some great fun with this using inexpensive tape recorders. Give your boy a recorder with the suggestion to goof around singing like some recording star he likes. It's hilarious.

Creatively Solving Problems

You should create six problem-solving outlets.

1. Give Me Three Solutions. During my graduate training, I worked in an experimental research setting. I'll never forget one professor who would ask for my opinions about his conclusions on his experiments. He'd say, "What do you think this result means?" and then he'd be quiet and let me blab. He'd continue, "What *else* could it mean?" Of course, I thought he was attempting to plumb the depths of my razor-like mind or get some free conclusions. Wrong. After we had cycled through the routing seven or eight times, I realized his angle: He was trying to open me up!

I press boys a lot. Like any good coach would, I ask them to perform. I'll now ask you to perform to the same standards. Whenever you face any problem, don't settle on a solution until you've created three alternatives. Make them all unique to provide you with the greatest latitude in selection. If you're having trouble thinking up three distinct solutions, don't stop. Keep asking yourself, Is there anything else I could do?

Insist on a similar arrangement with your boy. School problems, people problems, hobby problems, money woes—resist the urge to solve the mess for him, and encourage him to create three good ideas. Even urge him to think on it overnight.

2. How Would You Improve This? I often ask kids how they would change something to make it better. From sports equipment to salad dressings, I ask, "What would you do to make this better?" Expect the typical "I don't know" followed by suggestions about how it could be changed to be easier to hold, different color, different smell, and so on. That's focused creative thinking, and that's exactly what you want to prompt.

3. Experiment Wildly. Let your boy play with things, dissect things, and find out how machines and little beasties work. When I was a kid, I was always on the lookout for old radios and mechanical stuff to tear apart. Many friends would come over to my house to help me dismember the treasures because such operations were outlawed at their homes. What a shame! Let your boy find out how things work, and support inquiry. Carpe screwdriver (seize the screwdriver)!

My kids rarely come to me anymore to fix things because they know what I'm going to say: "Experiment with it." They know that's a license to try anything they want. I usually suggest they try to fix the thing, but if that's impossible, they are to tear it apart and learn from it. I advise that you not allow your boy to do this on electrical appliances unless you want him to become one. Anything else, from plants to bugs to old CDs, is fair game. Let serendipity be his teacher in creative experimentation.

4. Devise "What's Next?" Puzzles. They say you can't teach someone common sense. Yes, you can. It's done by helping boys learn to predict the immediate outcomes of their behavior. Common sense is nothing more than this. I treat my kids to these tutorials by constantly asking, "What would happen next after you did this?" What will happen next if you are playing catch with a baseball in front of a plate-glass window? What will happen next if you spend all your savings on baseball cards? These lessons are great practice in creative thinking

5. Draw Time Frames. I've devised an unusual method of teaching my kids about options called TimeFraming™. It works by re-creating scenarios inside small boxes drawn on a piece of paper. The boxes allow me to draw all the major sequences of a situation. I usually put arrows between the boxes to show how the action flowed. The last box is always the concluding scene of the event.

Once all the scenes are drawn (by either me or my son), I draw an arrow off the last box to an empty box. "What happened next?" I ask. That question is the first real step in a terrifically eye-opening creative journey.

I first used time framing with my son Jake after he experienced a common playground trauma. He had been punched by a kid named Jerry for what Jake claimed was no reason. After some brief questioning, I found out that just before Jerry hit my kid, Jake had "accidentally" kicked the ball and hit Jerry in the head. In my unique artistic way, I began to draw sequences. They looked something like those in Art 1.

ART 1

With more questioning, Jake was able to tell me what happened in the next frame: He started to cry and was embarrassed. I drew the frame in Art 2.

ART 2

I kept drawing box after box, with pictures of the major events that transpired as the rest of the day unfolded. I finally had about twenty separate boxes; in the final one Jake and I were drawing pictures on the couch.

I asked Jake to tell me during which frame he began to feel the situation going bad. Jake said the problem began when he hit Jerry with the ball. I disagreed, and to explain why, I drew several more time frames. They represented Jerry's and Jake's lives, and they looked like the ones in Art 3.

JERRY

JAKE

ART 3

I guessed that Jerry, who is underprivileged and uncared for, was having a bad day. He probably hadn't eaten breakfast and wasn't doing too well in school, so getting hit with the ball in the head just set him off. The situation disintegrated, I suggested, when the two boys' time frames collided.

Based on that insight, we drew *new* time frames with new behaviors that Jake could have used to change the entire event. These frames included Jake's finding out in the morning how Jerry was doing, being an encourager, apologizing for hitting Jerry, and not letting a punk destroy his day.

We even took this a step further. I asked Jake how he wanted to feel by the end of the day and then had him draw a picture of that feeling in a frame at the bottom of the page. Then I had him fill in four or five frames with things he could do before evening that would usher him to the final frame. He filled in all the frames with care. And the night ended just as Jake had drawn it.

6. Hold Point / Counterpoint Debates. Boys are not used to adults wanting to have friendly debates. Debates have negative connotations, and they will be difficult to lure your son to. Our society generally regards the basic human ability of debating as hostile confrontation to be avoided.

Set the rules ahead of time: Getting angry is absolutely forbidden, you have sixty seconds to present your case, Mom is the judge of the winner, and check your pistols at the door. Pick a topic, pick the position you want to defend, and take sixty seconds to think over your arguments. Ready, go!

Oversimplify this. Discuss allowances, artificial turf football, or the nutritional value of school lunches. Encourage your son to conjure up logical reasons to support his position, whatever it is, and help him do so if he has trouble. Help him draw valid conclusions, and remember, you win this debate only if your son wins. Do it as often as required to get your son in the habit of using his imagination to see many sides of issues. Defending them with brilliance will come later.

Using the brain can be accidental or well planned. I've found some procedures help boys learn to use their heads. It's fun for them, and the carryover from games into real life is natural.

ACTION TO TAKE

There is an excellent book called *Cool Tricks* by John Javna. Please find a copy and do some cool tricks with your son. If you cannot find a copy, make a Moebius Strip, and imagine what you might get in four sections.

CHAPTER 11

Good Boys . . . Bad Habits

GET TO THE POINT

What would happen if you let your boy do his thing, be totally free and uninhibited, and live any way he chose? Can you imagine what would happen? You might think his bedroom looks like he's living that way now, but imagine the quagmire it could become. Building good habits allows your son to live up to his potential. Bad habits will only hamper his rise to a quality place in life.

HEY, LITTLE GREEN TEETH, DID YOU KNOW YOU CAN WASH THOSE THINGS?

A few summers ago, I took my Cub Scout pack to a baseball game. It was a beautiful day, and we got terrific seats along the third baseline, over the home team dugout. I sat at the far end of a long row of seats, right next to a rough-looking bunch of kids. They were a little raucous, and as far as I could tell, there weren't any parents with them.

One little guy to my left was a wiggle worm, and he was eating everything he could get his hands on. Every so often he'd look up and peer at me through strings of matted hair and smile. His teeth were growing plants! I'd never seen such dirty teeth. I kept thinking that there was no way to get those things clean without chisels or power tools.

Have you ever seen a kid like that? Where were his parents? Did anyone care about him? The poor kid had three strikes against him, and he probably didn't even know it.

YOUR LIFE IS A COLLECTION OF YOUR HABITS

The boy in this story is probably not your son. You've taught your son some habits that keep him from being so pitiful. Were you taught any habits by your parents? Are there any you wish they had insisted upon but didn't? How would your life be different if you had some better habits?

These are eye-opening questions. Imagine if you had learned better discipline, more stick-to-itiveness, more promptness, and more decisiveness. Would life be different for you? Try this: Imagine having *less* of any good habit you have now. That's a scary thought!

For better or worse, every day leaps from a recipe called your personal habits. From the side of the bed you get up on to the way you brush your teeth to the way you drive to work to the way you drive home from work to the way you schedule your evening to the time you get back in bed, how much is pure routine, thoughtless, ingrained behaviors?

A GREAT HABIT = GOOD REASONS + GOOD REINFORCERS + GOOD REPETITION

If we understand habits from an engineering perspective we can learn how to build them good and strong. Sharp analysis reveals that habits have good reasons for being in operation. Habits generate rewards that you like. That's what keeps them happening, even if the habit—like smoking—is bad over the long term. According to the brain's natural law of economy, a habit needs to produce something positive and immediate, or it won't become a habit in the first place.

Though some behaviors provide a positive benefit, they don't yet become habits. Your brain is pretty smart, and it requires repetition for a behavior to be automated into a habit. How many reps? It varies. Crack cocaine becomes a habit in about ten minutes. Something without such a potent physical presence, like flossing your teeth, takes daily exposure for twenty-one days. The key is repetition, plain and simple.

Habit formations are relatively low-tech. There is no need to over-analyze it or overcoach you. Nature has organized your boy to continually seek behaviors that are helpful and, through self-generated rewards, to make the behaviors automatic.

I offer three suggestions. *First,* the level of difficulty in creating habits in boys increases with time. Like almost any other aspect of learning, the younger a boy is when he first learns something, the quicker it's picked up and the longer it stays. Once boys cross that thin line into self-consciousness, so many other factors enter into the mental mixture that the difficulty of learning new habits escalates steeply. Start your son early.

Second, recall from an earlier discussion the importance of consistent models. Boys pick up habits from adults and peer models with frightening ease. The last thing any boy needs is two significant adults arguing over the proprietary of one habit or another. It's very confusing. This problem usually crops up over habits of health, such as diet, exercise, alcohol, and tobacco. Do your level best to align the habits of the people your son contacts. You will do him a great favor by making the effort to have all the adults in his life present a unified front. It reduces his confusion and dramatically improves the chances of his adopting the healthy habits he needs.

Third, the biggest problem you will face in building habits is not creating habits but deciding what is a good habit for your son and what is not.

Good and Bad Habits

If you had been raised independent of any outside forces (such as schools, churches, parents, and teachers), your habits and your life would have followed a jagged line of least resistance. Your habits would have formed along the lines of your comfort zone, wherever that happened to be. You'd have as many habits as you do now but for radically different reasons.

Why isn't your life directed by every whim and pleasure? Because you have developed a more disciplined group of habits that force your life to a higher level. The habits deny you a little instant pleasure now in exchange for the promise of a lot more in the future.

We call these good habits. They force you to do things you wouldn't do naturally. Good habits align with prevailing standards of success, propriety, efficiency, class, good taste, and sociability. Examples might include proper speech, deference to authorities, and politeness in the presence of strangers. These habits have likely served you well, but how far could you have gone with a *better* list of habits?

Give Him What You Wish You Had

Wouldn't you love to give the good habits you lack to your son? You are in a perfect spot to judge what the missing habits are. Better personal habits will help your boy become exceptional for at least three reasons. First, most of the good achievements in life require more than accidental effort. They require *disciplined* effort.

For most boys, the first encounter with disciplined effort is for a prize worthy of the effort: a bicycle! Crashing into trees, scraping knees, and scared to death, but deeply moved to get up and try again. If only we could transfer such disciplined effort to cleaning rooms!

Second, a disciplined boy with good personal habits stands out in the crowd. He not only can be his best, but he has the means to be in a class by himself.

Third, having good personal habits makes learning the rest of the

Renaissance traits much easier. All the personal traits of Renaissance men hang together and interact like complex mental scaffolding. Good habits create their own internal support network, pushing the scaffolding skyward. Good habits push a person's life upward whether he intends it or not, even in situations when his focused efforts fade or dissolve.

It's called automatic excellence. I know one fellow who falls into more success in an hour than I do in a year! I've made this friend the focus of great study, for I wish for what this guy does. I've found his only oddity is that his habits, being well ingrained and perfectly automatic, consistently put him in successful situations. These habits, including being on time, returning phone calls, tackling big problems head-on, and talking with hundreds of people, guarantee his success. With this set of habits, he literally can't be stopped—and by setting high standards for your boy and making the standards habit, excellence can become automatic for him too.

Exercise forbearance, consistency, and love as you work with your son. Building new habits will require time and effort, so settle in and begin.

FIVE SUCCESS ZONES

I want to urge you to build a series of habits that fall within five distinct zones.

1. Manners

Men of the New Renaissance must be well mannered. I suggest the creation of four specific habits with respect to manners: personal greetings, introductions, table manners, and phone manners.

These manners will be useful to your boy forever. *Personal greetings* are a terrific example. Show your son how to shake hands, look people straight in the eye, and say, "It's nice to meet you." I work particularly hard on volume of the voice and strength of the grip: "Squeeze the hand you are shaking and talk loud." Practice this every day.

Introductions can be taught the same way. My kids are always bringing someone new into the house, so there are ample chances for them to say, "Dad, this is Jimmy Scaredstiff. Jimmy, this is my dad, Bill Beausay." I insist that they use this pattern because it's efficient and the standard practice. Teach your son to conduct introductions this way or perhaps a variation of your own. The point is to allow your boy to develop under your tutelage and get comfortable with the slight rigor it imposes.

Table manners aren't so cut and dried. I know that all families have their routines around the table, and I don't want to tamper with your traditions. Just make sure you have some, for your son needs predictability in his life, and this is one place where it is easy to apply. Strive to have the family eat at least one meal a day together. The table historically has been the place where families gather to talk, share experiences, discuss problems, and share some downtime together. It's not asking too much to turn off the TV during meals, refuse to take phone calls, stay at the table till everyone's finished, use eating utensils (properly), and be thankful for the food and time together.

I know I probably sound like Ward Cleaver, but hear me out. I find that kids made to be grateful get grateful. Expose him to warmth, acceptance, and appreciation within your home, in contrast to the desperately cold world outside.

As for *phone manners,* speaking loudly and firmly, saying "please" and "thank you," taking accurate messages, and repeating phone numbers are just a few suggestions.

Today, it is practically impossible to get away with poor communication skills of any kind. Poor communication skills prevent many people from advancing in jobs and careers. So teach, correct, and encourage.

Supervised use of 800 numbers is great experience for talking with strangers. If you exercise care in explaining who pays for these calls and the responsibility that demands, this can be a wonderful learning experience.

When Lamborghini came out with the new Diablo car, my older son,

Jake, was in love. I got the 800 number of a dealer, and I had Jake call him with a list of questions we prepared ahead of time. Jake told him he was a young entrepreneur (he has a paper route) and he had some money to burn (I told him I'd rather he get a Diablo than more baseball cards). The dealer was very kind to him and fielded all his questions. Chutzpah!

Teach your son about the world with the phone, and teach him to use the phone fearlessly.

2. Chivalry

This quality is going to be big in the New Renaissance! Get your son in gear for it now by building habits of courtesy, bravery, and helpfulness. How should you do that? Of the zones in which we build habits, this one requires the most modeling. And the model is you!

Courtesy is taught by instruction and repetition. Who should your boy be courteous to? Everyone. "Please" and "thank you" are acceptable. "Yes, sir" and "no, sir," "yes, ma'am" and "no, ma'am," are the standards of excellence. In addition to teaching him what to say, instruct him on the proper time to apply courtesy.

When a boy speaks with this sort of respect, he is treated differently from everyone else. Because it's so unusual, your son can quickly cut sharp lines of impression with persons he meets. To teach courtesy, run through the wording a few times, model it for him before you meet people, and ask that he talk that way.

Build *bravery* with everyday heroism. Your son can perform a small heroic selfless act a day. The Cub Scouts break this down further by telling boys to do a good deed every day. They even have a ceremony where boys are turned upside down by two adults and awarded a badge. When they are righted, the badge appears upside down, and they are not allowed to turn it over until they have done a good deed. The hardest part of this quest for any Scout (or other boy for that matter) is seeing opportunities for everyday heroism.

Show your son the chances he has to help others—whether it's standing up for what's right in an argument, helping a friend carry books, or opening the door for someone. Doing small good deeds or heroic acts is self-reinforcing once started. You can jump-start the process by suggesting one idea every day and rewarding him with a hug, a pat on the back, or a big smile. Or you can stay watchful for spontaneous acts of bravery and then buy him an ice cream.

A good friend of mine, Bob Shook, has written many books on building character and living effectively. When his boys were younger, he wanted them to build heroism and character, so he made a pact with them. Whenever they went to a dance, they had to ask the shyest and most withdrawn girl to dance first. The boys complied and created some wonderful memories for some very shy girls. Heroism means a lot to those who are in need.

Helpfulness is different from everyday heroism. Helpfulness is something you find to do around the house. It doesn't take genius to spot when someone around the house is in trouble, and then jump to help! Yet, how many of us have struggled with grocery bags at the front door while the kids sat and watched television, or how many times has the phone gone unanswered because nobody would get it?

Once I saw something that perhaps you can relate to. I walked out the front door of my house and saw a mother and a son wrestling on the ground across the street! (I knew they were mother and son because they were my neighbors.) Being a good neighbor, I ran inside and watched from between the curtains. Hair and fingernails and pieces of clothing were flying out of this nasty ball of humanity. I later found out the little brouhaha started when the mother was lecturing the boy about cleaning up a mess he had made in front of the television. He said the four words that ignite seething rage inside all parents of ungrateful and unresponsive boys: *Can I go now?*

Helpfulness is a tough habit to build because you want your son to have a desire to help. You want it to spring naturally within your boy without twisting his arm. Let me suggest two approaches.

First, tell your boy what you expect. Most kids who are by nature unhelpful have never had their parents clearly explain what they expect. Remember that most boys are not aware of much anyway, let alone when to jump up and be helpful. Tell your boy clearly what you expect, and ask him to look for moments and opportunities to pitch in and help.

Second, build within him smaller qualities that add up to helpful behavior: attentiveness to what's going on around him, appreciation for other people's needs, sensitivity about family rules, appreciation that sometimes life is chaotic and everyone needs to help, and so on. Build up each of these qualities individually in little ways by creating real-life experiences. Let the experiences become his instructor. The combined weight of these individual qualities make the probability of spontaneous helpfulness much greater.

How do you create real-life experiences? Say, for example, you wanted your son to appreciate other people's needs. Give him a bag of groceries, and ask him to stand outside the screen door with nobody around to open it. Let him stand there for sixty seconds. That's all it will take. Ask him how it feels. Find out if he would want other people to be in trouble and have nobody around to help. Don't do this when you're mad about his thoughtlessness. Otherwise, the lesson will be considered punishment and won't have the effect of educating him.

3. Interaction with Girls

This might not appear to be habit-making material, but during this stage, boys learn important habits of interacting with girls. Parental attitudes at home, school experiences, and neighborhood friendships form the interactive elements of this habit.

You've learned about the changes in boys as they grow before and after the onset of self-consciousness. We find interesting differences in the treatment of girls prior to and after this change. Pretransition boys (prior to the eight- to ten-year-old range) don't typically have prejudices against girls unless modeled by an older boy. Around the time of transition, biases and mistreatment become epidemic. Some may call it normal.

However normal it may be, I prefer to think that we need to intervene in the feelings of boys toward girls.

Interestingly enough, boys seem to need enemies. They need people to team up against, to fight against, to unite in opposition to, and so forth. Girls are natural adversaries. They look different, are typically more academically inclined as a group, are more mature, and often gain preferential treatment from adults. There are many good reasons to hate them in BoyThink.

How can you encourage your boy to treat girls properly? *First,* appreciate that you are laying the groundwork for something that might not necessarily show up immediately. All habits (especially those relating to treating girls properly) are learned slowly and must be massaged deeply into the life of your son. Set your expectations on a long-term, consistent daily effort.

Second, teach your boy to interact properly with his mother. He should rehearse treating Mother with deference and respect, and he should learn the fine, unboylike qualities of touching gently and complimenting. Mom will love it.

Third, build the habit of controlling the tongue—specifically, no verbal abuse, no foul language, and no references to unusual physical characteristics. It is easy to learn to be quiet, and that often is the best thing a boy can do around girls. The old "if you can't say something nice, don't say anything" message applies nicely here.

Fourth, when your boy goofs up and is unnecessarily rude to a girl, make him apologize. I've been very surprised in my conversations with boys to discover the number of them who agree that they deserve to make restitutions or apologies for mistakes they've made. Most boys will even tell you that they deserve to be punished for some of the mistakes they make! Apologizing for goof-ups should be automatic for your son.

But he won't learn it automatically or naturally. In my experience I've found that the best way to teach this is head-on. You could go to great lengths to help your boy understand the feelings of girls and get him to relate to the experience of being humiliated by a knuckleheaded boy. Save your effort till later. At this point, help him learn that rudeness isn't going to be tolerated toward anyone, and he needs to apologize immediately if he violates the rule. Teach this as a way of life.

Fifth, explain to your boy what *you* expect. You don't need me to tell you exactly how to make your son conduct himself with girls. You have your opinions, but perhaps you need to underscore them. I have offered a few ideas here, but the bottom line is, you must decide what standards you want your son to perform to, and then make it a goal for him to attain. Write it out; draw pictures; rehearse; do whatever you like. Provide precise definitions and clear directions.

Ask your son to assume leadership in this area and develop an idea of what he thinks is proper. Whenever one of my charges is mean to a girl when I'm around, I separate him from the pack, and we have a talk. I'm usually most interested in finding out what he expects from himself.

In most cases, boys have clear ideas of how to treat girls, but due to high concentrations of peer pressure, they buckle and act in ways contrary to their beliefs. Encourage and persuade your boy to stick to his guns and do what he feels is best. A boy needs that vote of confidence and persuasion from an adult, especially about those things he feels deeply but is embarrassed to admit in public.

4. Personal Care and Hygiene

I once had the pleasure of meeting a real prince. He was the son of a wealthy Arab family, heir to a veritable fortune. I knew he must be some sort of prince by just observing him. He was short, but his trained posture made him look seven feet tall. His eyes were clear, he was dressed to the nines, and his every movement was made with precision. Polished and regal in every way, he defined what good grooming and hygiene can produce. By comparison, I felt like a slouched, fat American mutt!

I learned a lot of things from the young prince. The most important was that care and attention to hygiene and personal appearance matter. They can have an impact on others far beyond what you know.

Consider teaching your son habits in three areas: personal grooming, good posture, and proper clothing.

Like the other habits, keep the list of what you want to do simple. List things you want your son to do daily, and post that list in his bedroom or on the bathroom wall. That list should include taking a bath or shower, brushing teeth, flossing, combing hair, cleaning fingernails, washing the face in the morning, and using deodorant as needed.

The list we have posted in the house shows drawings of the kids doing each of these activities. The pictures are intentionally funny, and the kids frequently refer to which picture they need to do. The guiding principle here is the same as for other ideas in this book: Does the effort you put forth to take care of yourself represent your best effort? If your son can answer yes, and you agree, fine. Of the habits that require daily commitment, I suggest that you make these top priorities if not for your son, then for the guy who has to sit by him at the next baseball game!

There are sound health reasons for standing with good posture. Much like eating roughage reduces the risk of lower gastrointestinal problems, maintaining good posture reduces the risk of back problems in later life. If these reasons are not enough, a boy with great posture looks like a prince and feels better about himself.

Build good posture by reminding your son to walk tall, and make frequent measurements of his height. Mark the doorposts! Explain to him the value in standing straight, and maybe even point out people you see in public who are good examples.

Two little fellows in our neighborhood are very small. They've told me how difficult it is to play with the other boys because of their size. I encourage them by saying, "You're as tall as you think you are!" and I know the little boys take such encouragement seriously. If they strut off like Napoleon, I feel that they've learned the truth—that height is in the head!

Clothing and dressing necessitate a series of habits. I am not into clothes, and I don't believe it's crucial to spend lots of money on them or to have the latest fashions. Quality clothes, well maintained, are just fine. Inexpensive clothes, well maintained, are fine. Maintenance is the crucial factor, and that should be a team effort. Make sure your son understands good clothing maintenance: putting things away, learning the difference between doorknobs and hangers, and knowing how to work a washing machine.

I guarantee that if your son does the laundry occasionally, he won't throw his clothes on the floor as often. A washing machine is easy to run, so any six-year-old can learn not to put a red cotton shirt in with the whites.

Boys, particularly those after the transition to self-consciousness, will have their favorites they will want to wear constantly. That's fine. Just make sure your boy keeps them clean. Soon enough the novelty wears off (with luck, before the knees), and he'll move onto the next favorite.

Make your boy responsible for how he looks very early on, and the habit will stay with him after you're no longer around to tell him how good he looks!

5. TMWOD (Time, Money, Work, Ownership, and Decisiveness)

I lump these together for a specific reason. When I decided to write a chapter about habits, I wanted to summarize and discuss certain patterns of behavior that lead to success. In my observations of winners, it is clear that an "80/20" rule is in effect: 80 percent of the success created by 20 percent of the habits! The consistent winners are the ones who automatically perform these few behaviors with absolute regularity.

Think of *time* as a commodity. It's of great value to adults, due to our limited supply. Boys, having a large supply of time, steeply devalue its worth. They need to be taught habits of wise consumption of probably the single most precious resource they own. Don't go off the deep end on this. This is the time to begin teaching your boy about wisely using time, not making him into a little clock-watcher. You do that by instituting daily rituals that are coordinated with a clock. Getting up, cleaning his room, doing chores, and watching television are a few of the opportunities you have to connect his activities with a clock. If you've accomplished this connection, you've done your son a sweet service. Consider this job done, except for one thing.

Give your son some time completely to himself. No appointments, no schedules, nothing. Always remember that above all, he is a boy, and he deserves to act without the rigidity of karate lessons, violin lessons, practice, and other such schedules. It is possible to overbook your kid. Give him a break. Leave him time to do what he wants.

Let's talk about *money*. Let's talk specifically about the difference in money the boy gets and the money the boy earns. Money the boy gets is often called an allowance. Allowances can create trouble in families. Allowances should be given for many good reasons, but amounts and required tasks are open to debate. I know parents who have developed elaborate point systems with rewards and cash bonuses. Then again, I've seen parents doling out double-digit allowances weekly for nothing! I grew up in a home where allowances were random, depending on how much was in my mom's pockets.

Allowances work best when they model something in the real world. If in the real world you work for cash, do so at home. If in your real world, you get money for nothing other than smiling, do the same thing at home. Households that dole out money based on waking up risk what the government has discovered about entitlement programs: If you don't work to get it, you won't appreciate it or work to get more. Make certain that allowances reflect life.

How much to give? Ask neighbors and friends how much is customary and reasonable in your town, and then decide on an amount that you can comfortably pay each week. The average among those I've asked is between three and ten dollars per week. Set it up however you please, but make an allowance a matter of education rather than a birthright.

Now, let's talk about earning money. This is, of course, related to work, and it should be. Entrepreneurial ventures and hard physical labor should always be encouraged in your boy. Be sure to teach the value of "making" money versus "getting" money.

My dad is a genuine character. When I was a boy, he was always arranging little businesses for me to run to make some serious moola! I handed out flyers, trying to get a leaf-raking business to happen. I painted addresses on curbs. Once he even suggested selling imported Israeli panty hose!

Get your boy to start something: a business or a real job. Most of the businesses he will start will be of the labor variety or the sales variety. Labor jobs include having a paper route, shoveling snow, raking leaves, mowing lawns, chasing rabbits out of people's gardens, and so on.

While I'm on the topic of paid physical labor, it seems sensible to me to encourage your son to learn a wage-earning skill. Granted, he might be a bit young to learn to weld or pour cement, but having a wage-earning skill means he will never go hungry. He'll always, throughout his life, be able to get a job doing his skill for real money. Teaching him a skill might be equivalent to feeding him for years into the future.

Sales jobs are a little different. Though trades can be mastered only when boys get older, salesman-like activities can be launched now. Lemonade stands can be frustrating but educational. You might want to attempt some more realistic commerce: Buy a box of candy bars, sell them at marked-up prices, and keep the profit.

He could sell anything. Encourage him to have a bedroom sale and unload some of his junk. Sell some old stuff in newspaper classifieds. Get him involved in a Junior Achievement group so he'll learn all sorts of ways to sell products. If he doesn't think he can sell, give him a copy of *The Greatest Salesman in the World* by Og Mandino. It's a great story that an older boy should memorize.

There is no more human activity than *work*. Historically, it started at birth and ended at death, but trade unions and federal courts have intervened. The word *workaholic* has further driven the value into disrepute. Nowadays, work for most people doesn't it start till around the age of eighteen and ends sometime in the sixties. Work has changed from being life to being part of life.

I'm reminded of the story my good friend Harvey Boston, noted motivational speaker, told. Harvey had gone to visit a very successful man to divine the secret of his wealth. The wise older man looked at young Harvey and said, "It's simple. I plan half the day, and I spend another half working on the plan." Harvey said, "Yahoo! You mean all I have to do is plan four hours a day and I'll be rich?" The older man smiled slightly and sadly shook his head. "No, son," he said. "It was plan twelve hours a day and work the plan twelve hours a day."

Now it's obviously ill advised to work twenty-four hours a day. But it's equally silly to leave your son work-free. If you make your son do chores now, he will discover that work is more than idle exercise or punishment. Hard work gives an appreciation for real life, and it teaches all sorts of lessons unavailable by any other means.

When I discuss *ownership,* I'm referring to being responsible with things and respecting personal property. If he works and puts forth some effort, he will accumulate money, which inevitably translates into personal junk. Much like teaching him the care of clothing, go the extra mile to make him personally responsible for caring for toys, bikes, radios, skateboards, and so on. Our society encourages disposability, no matter how alive the ecological movement remains. We are a society overbuilt on the foundations of convenience and "throw it away if it breaks." Do your boy a favor and teach him the proper care of things and the value of restoration—fixing things. These are values he will fall back on if his life ever lies shattered about him.

Encourage your son to make good, prompt decisions. The roots of procrastination grow deeply during boyhood, primarily because boys are allowed to put off decisions. Making decisions can be fearful, creating hesitation. The habit of *decisiveness* allows your son to experience how easy making choices can be. Start this habit by insisting that he choose between two things. Ask him to make choices about two easy options. What does he want for dinner, meat or nonmeat? Don't let him off the hook with an "I don't care." Where does he want to sit in the car, in the front or in the back? How would he like his clothes folded, in halves or in quarters?

What you want to accomplish is decisiveness rather than procrastination. Make a decision *now* without putting it off. Good decision making is an art form in itself.

THE VERY BEST YOU CAN BE FOR YOUR BOY

. . . is the very best you can be for yourself. You have heard me echo the theme of being your best, so let me mention this: Your boy is more moldable and changeable today than he will ever be for the rest of his life. He's watching you. Do you want him to be like you in every detail, good and bad?

If not, take this challenge to push yourself up a notch on the class and self-discipline scales. This reminds me of a story I heard. An aide to Henry Kissinger was asked to create a report on a developing global situation. The aide went away and returned the next week with a report packaged in a nice folder. After a day, Dr. Kissinger called the aide back and asked if that was the best he could do. The aide, being a little intimidated, responded that he thought he could improve it.

A week later the aide delivered an updated report. Once again after a day, Kissinger returned the report with instructions to improve it. The aide pulled out all the stops and created a beautiful report with more graphics and more detailed analysis. After he delivered it again, he was asked again if it was the best he could do.

The aide was completely exasperated. One last time he focused and polished and groomed the report to a higher quality. It was the best he could possibly do. He had no more to give. He personally took the report into Kissinger and said, "Dr. Kissinger, you've asked me to revise this report many times. Each time I've made it a little better, but this is absolutely the best I can make it."

Kissinger replied, "Well, if that is the best you can make it, I'll read it."

Give this your all. Become a living example of a class act. Become a person your son would want to follow. Just as you can teach your son great habits with just seconds of work per day, so can you transform *yourself* into the picture of excellence with a little effort. It takes so little time to rise above the mob. Do it!

ACTION TO TAKE Start off slowly. Pick one habit and create it slowly, through repetition, for the next couple of weeks. Keep your efforts simple and direct. No fancy stuff. Good habits create an atmosphere where good attitudes can flourish.

CHAPTER 12

"You Got an Attitude, Boy"

 If it can be influenced in you, you can influence it in your son. What follows is an improved method of handling one of parenthood's deepest quandaries.

QUASARS

Every field of endeavor has problems that are way out on the fringe. They're mysteries that for lack of sufficient breadth of knowledge are too remote to unravel. The experts can only look off in the distance and wonder.

In astronomy, the most distant and mysterious objects in the universe are quasars. They are perplexing objects literally at the outer edges of the universe. Quasars are enormous sources of energy, but that's about all we know. Whatever quasars are, astronomers think they hold some key to understanding how all things work.

In psychology, attitudes and motivations are the quasars. Though much has been written about them both, not much is reliably known. They constantly twinkle in our daily lives, as if to taunt and play with our reason. We don't—perhaps can't—know much about them. Don't expect any breakthrough soon.

"I'VE HAD IT UP TO
HERE WITH THIS ATTITUDE"

Have you ever been in a store and seen a harangued parent with a Neanderthal child? Not too long ago I was in a supermarket, witnessing one such duo. It was vaudeville! The little kid was sliding around the floor, screaming and kicking, and his dad was trying to reason with him. It was so bad I almost walked up to the guy and asked him whether it would be all right if I spanked his kid for him. I cautiously approached the boy, who was all of about five, and I glared down at him. He was one of those kids who glared back. He was a real weasel! I should have walked away, but I couldn't.

"What's your name, son?" I asked.

"Junior," he grunted. (These kids are always "juniors.")

"You don't look like you like this store too much," I said.

"Only stupid people like this store!" he snapped.

A wise guy, huh? I thought. "Where are you from, Junior?"

"Earth," he said.

I think that's what he said. I was too busy backing away trying to put out the fire in my nostrils!

Parents' most frequent complaint is about their boys' bad attitudes. This presenting complaint of bad attitudes isn't the real problem, though. The real problem is the disillusionment parents feel because the best effort they've put forward has been ineffective in changing their sons. They lash out in frustration, blaming attitude problems for their own inadequacy. We need to banish this misplaced blame and give parents the knack for changing their boys' attitudes and leapfrog over the aggravation represented by bad attitudes!

We must define attitudes in such a way that they are found to be adjustable. Don't bother Webster. You're dealing with a quasar. In defining an almost complete unknown, you must first make some informed guesses and see if they hold water in practice. If they fail to help in any way, go back to the drawing board.

I've saved you the time and trouble of drawing boards. I'll share four hypotheses in defining fixable attitudes, and I'll suggest ways to apply them. These are potent, and they allow you leverage in altering your effectiveness with intransigent attitudes.

Hypothesis #1: There Are Two Species of Attitudes

Core attitudes are the orientations present at conception. Our understanding of what kids are born with is far more sophisticated today than ten years ago. Science is making tremendous leaps in knowledge about genetically programmed qualities like shyness, brain activity (a baby's brain is twice as active as an adult's), differences between newborn males and females in visual perception and movement control, and auditory perception. There is mounting evidence that many traits we believed were learned are actually genetically prescribed. The possibility of finding still more genetically created qualities is obvious.

These core attitudes form your basic orientation to life. If you were a computer, these would be called your defaults, the orientations you always return to. Core attitudes run the range from optimistic, energetic, feisty, lighthearted, and scrappy to deeply brooding, discontented, introverted, morose, overly tolerant, and the like. The key identifier is their enduring, automatic appearance when nothing else is occurring to set off a more spontaneous emotional reaction.

Transient attitudes, the second species, are more like emotional reactions that appear and disappear quickly. Their cycle can be from seconds to days, and they can emerge in many forms. These attitudes are very noticeable and have as their earmark the quality of impermanence: joyful, playful, excited, distractable, blue, talkative, contrary, fickle, indecisive, self-pitying, depressed, and so on. They are the ones drawing most of the ire and disaffection of parents. They're also easier to change than core attitudes.

Hypothesis #2: Attitudes Don't Always Operate Logically

Trying to investigate attitudes can be maddening work. At times it's like trying to understand the thinking of tornadoes! Attitudes are utterly capricious. Trying to use logic to understand them is futile. Illogic bewilders logic.

What controls attitudes? Perhaps biochemistry. Freud did say that eventually everything about human behavior would be explained through chemistry. Maybe they come and go due to spiritual causes. Perhaps an undiscovered level of mental-emotional function? Like questions about quasars, these questions are open to speculation.

Trying to sort out attitudes by understanding them can be like pouring slow-acting acid on your resolve; you end up scalding your own attitude! Forget the reasons and causes for attitudes. What matters is having the optimism and method to change them if they are unacceptable to you or your family.

Hypothesis #3: Boys Aren't Aware of Their Attitudes

You may know that you can cook a frog without its knowledge (or permission). Since a frog is cold-blooded, its body temperature rises with the heat of the water. Put it in a pot of water and slowly bring the water to a boil and it'll never notice. Presto! Cooked frog.

Boys, especially the younger ones, are cold-blooded with respect to their attitudes. They cook and simmer in their attitudes, but they are almost totally unaware of them. Adult-style self-consciousness and experience are required to recognize the temperature of the water. Can anything be done until maturity steps to the rescue? Does it do any good to talk to your son about these matters?

Yes, you can influence attitudes in the meantime, and yes, you should talk to your son about the situation. Don't expect him to understand, though. Recall our lessons from an earlier chapter: If he can't see, hear, touch, taste, or smell it, it won't reckon in his head. Still, it always makes sense to try, for it might connect.

Hypothesis #4: Attitudes Are Prime Motivators

Motivation: another quasar. We talk about motivation as if we might know what it is, but what really makes people get up and go? This is another Nobel prize question. About all we can say for sure is that within us is a spark plug that, when charged in the presence of flammable thinking, will explode, propelling us into movement. That isn't a very specific analogy, but it may be the best we can infer.

Each person seems to have an idiosyncratic formula for this combustible thinking. *Attitudes* are the bowl in which we mix the basic ingredients and without which not much motivation happens. Prevailing moods and perspectives create the possibility of action.

That is why I call attitudes *prime motivators*. Without the basic structure of proper attitude, getting even the most capable person motivated to act is practically impossible. Conversely, with the right structure, a seemingly talentless person can do the impossible.

GIVE ME A FOCAL MOMENT

Allow me to sharply focus on what we are about to do. We know that attitudes exist. We know that for an assortment of reasons, we like some attitudes and dislike others. We intuitively understand that proper (good) attitudes allow growth and that improper (bad) attitudes suppress. And now, we have four working hypotheses about the activity of attitudes that suggest means of influencing them.

We will be practicing methods derived from the four hypotheses. Hypothesis #1 (two species of attitudes) suggests that some attitudes are easier to change than others. Hypothesis #2 (no logic) suggests that what you might be certain will work might fail, and that what makes no sense at all might work miracles. Hypothesis #3 (not conscious of attitudes) suggests that if we can be creative in showing boys specifically how their attitudes affect them, perhaps their very dim speck of self-consciousness can be roused to greater activity. Hypothesis #4 (prime motivators) is our purest intention for wanting to build good attitudes in the first place: so our boys can feel the exhilaration and pleasure of self-motivation.

The Outside-In Approach

We are struggling to build boy masterpieces with crude instruments. We can do it. In changing the attitudes of adults, standard counseling procedure suggests change from the inside out. That means talking to them about their thoughts and dreams, encouraging them to get all the bad stuff out in the open, and offering analysis and advice.

This approach doesn't work so well with kids. When I was first in college, I participated in a church-sponsored children's program at a local orphanage. I was a gung ho college sophomore, and the pro bono counseling arrangement was great experience. There were many broken little hearts in that place.

I loved being with those kids, hearing what they thought and trying to help in any way I could. I did what was natural, trying to get some of the tougher children to open up, but to no avail. The harder I tried to draw them out, the more puzzled they became. They didn't know what I was trying to get at.

Some boys respond well to the drawing-out approach, but most don't have any ability to clearly understand what you are trying to do. More often it's necessary to apply some creative action from the outside in. This means inducing certain outside conditions for proper attitudes to form inside your son.

Before I explain how this works, I need to explain how it fails. Transient attitudes cause boys most of their problems. That's good because they're easier to alter anyway. Core attitudes are a much darker mystery. They embody an innately sovereign orientation to life and quickly repel any effort to change them. The best fixes I've ever found are of a spiritual nature far removed from the feeble efforts of men or science.

Chapter 17 discusses this dimension at length. For now, tune your attention to successfully interacting with transient attitudes and the rancor they impart.

This outside-in approach does several things. *First,* it directs your son to healthy and satisfying attitudes he didn't know he had in the first place. *Second,* it puts you in the driver's seat. It makes you an integral member of your boy's psyche and provides reasoned approaches to helping your son. *Third,* it teaches your son to see attitude change as something positive and fun. *Fourth,* though core attitudes are distant and perplexing quasars, I believe that helping your son develop great transient attitudes somehow marinates the tough and unchanging core attitudes in new possibilities.

The Outside In: The Three-Pronged Fork

There are no less than three prongs to poke and provoke new attitude growth from outside your boy: (1) assigning attitudes, (2) body sculpting, and (3) praxis modeling. Each is doable.

Kids are remarkably flexible, and they can conform themselves to many different attitude requests without the slightest difficulty. And their attitudes really change. Telling your kids to "get happy," "be alert," "get excited," and so on is very effective.

I call the opportunity afforded this fact *assigning attitudes.* Most parents have failed in changing their boys' attitudes because they haven't told or asked their sons to change an attitude. These parents have failed to suggest new attitudes to use. They've bought in to this New Age caper that tells parents to let their kids go to develop freely and unobstructed. That is highly dangerous and does nothing to stretch your son's potential.

When I sense boys struggling due to an improper attitude, I suggest an attitude they need to have. If they need to get light and happy, I tell them so. I worked with a little boy who was a chronic frowner. His parents told me that he was always unhappy and mean-looking. I told the little guy that whenever he came to see me, he had to "wear a smile" or I would be allergic to him. Every time he frowned, I'd start to sneeze, so the only thing I could do to stop sneezing was to make him smile. That was easily done, for nobody had ever told him to lighten up and smile. I'd call him "smiley boy" and "rubber lips" and "the giggle master." He loved it, and he caught the attitude of happiness in a very short time.

Boys don't always respond so readily. Nothing works all the time. However, boys absorb a terrific amount if we offer a suggestion as a legitimate course of action. Never force those ideas, and always try to suggest what is appropriate.

When my son Zac rode his bike with me as I ran, we talked about running over ants, we spit on trees, I pushed him if he got tired, and he slapped me on the rear end when he could reach. Once he ran over a tall curb because he wasn't paying attention. He got banged around pretty good and started to cry. I wasn't in a sympathetic mood and made him keep riding despite his tears. The only thing that struck me funny about it was that he didn't get mad at me.

Later, after giving the incident some thought I told him I would understand if he were mad at me. I admitted that I had acted foolishly. My purpose in doing this was to admit my error and to give him room for a little righteous anger, which, frankly, I deserved. His little eyes sparkled and danced at the opportunity. In a respectful and potent way, he lit into me about my thoughtlessness. He did it very well, and I told him so. His analysis of my overly tough actions was first-rate. Boys can do anything with some encouragement.

Body sculpting builds on the observation that specific body postures get connected over time to specific feelings and attitudes. When people are depressed, they tend to slump and slouch, walk slowly, and have droopy faces. People who are happy walk erectly, with a peppy gait, and have a more open, congenial look. Each of us develops very early in life specific postures for each specific attitude we experience.

That's what makes it possible for you to look at others and almost feel what they feel. That's what makes you so readable to others—posture and gait and emotions that are written all over you. Go out in public and attune your senses to how someone must be feeling to walk that way. Practice this as you drive around. You'll become skillful, for example, at guessing who's happy and who's grumpy. Wave at the happy ones and honk at the grumps!

Now for some fun! You can change a boy's internal atmosphere by changing his external posturing. If for whatever reason your son's in some attitudinal orbit that you want him out of, make him change his posture, shift the way he sits, alter the speed with which he walks and talks, comb his hair, cross his eyes, put on earrings, or do anything! Change some external parameter. Like the example of the links in the chain, alter one link, and the whole chain must readjust.

Try this experiment: It's almost impossible to be depressed when you walk quickly with your shoulders thrown back, spine erect, head high, breathing deeply. It's an instant depression cure. On the other hand, it is equally difficult to remain buoyant and happy when you sit slouched, looking at the floor, expressionless, breathing slowly. Try it. Go now, and try each posture. This approach to shifting an internal state is thoroughly profound.

The most amazing thing about applying body sculpting is how quickly and accurately it works. The biggest challenge is to make the changes persist. You do that by reminding your son as often as necessary to repeat the postures associated with the attitude he wishes to maintain. You can walk up to him and do it manually if you must. I often jump on my kids and pull their lips up into a smile.

I've had to deal with many miserable kids. My personal pledge is that I'm not going to stand by and let them be miserable when it is in my power to do something. I've been creative with my trickery. I often tell the little sourballs that I'm going to shrink into a miniature body and sit on their shoulders, laughing at them. I make them look at their shoulder and see me sitting there, giggling and making faces. Every time they are really feeling surly or cross, they will see me perched there, blowing in their faces and telling them jokes. That always makes them smile!

One caution: You will be tempted to use an outside-in approach on adults. It's quite effective, but the rules of application are much different. Most adults won't let you grab their lips. They won't allow you close enough to them to make any meaningful suggestions about posture or physical expression, either. If they are willing participants, you can make some great attitudinal shifts. If they're not, you can only stand by and consider what could have been.

Praxis modeling is a vibrant way to influence a boy. *Praxis* is of Greek derivation, meaning roughly "to learn by example." I am not going to ask you to model attitudes for your son in any conventional way. Conventional ways are much too sloppy. I will, however, suggest two ideas. First, the dynamic nonverbal exchanges between you and your son have an erratic, arbitrary nature that you must control. Second, you cannot hope to lead anybody to a place you have never been.

When you recognize an attitude your son needs, you must magnify that attitude in your actions. You would be very disturbed to find out how little your son can really describe about you. A boy doesn't automatically pick up all your traits and values. You may very well have a trait that you feel is prominent and desirable but that your son does not even see. What he sees may have little connection to what you think you show him. Praxis modeling requires that you focus, align, and energize your attitudes along a direction that is unmistakably clear to your son.

You can accomplish this by making your important attitudes more distinct. You might want to limit your modeling to three striking attitudes. Explain their value, and demonstrate how your son might start witnessing them as they arise from you in real-life situations.

He'll need to start spending some time with you for the purpose of watching. Your part is to make sure the attitudes spring from you as you said they would. If you have any doubts, get yourself together before you open your mouth. Your son will teach whatever you *praxis* for him, so be sure you know what that is.

Praxis modeling provides a way for your son to know unmistakably what attitudes he is supposed to be seeing. Though it works best with older boys (after the eight- to ten-year transition), it's a powerful tool to mold desirable attitudes for a boy of any age.

IF HE KNOWS HE IS LOVED

In my many years as a counselor, I never met a boy who enjoyed being stuck in an unhappy attitude, core or transient. Boys might bite and scream and be foul, but they do not like the misery bad attitudes produce.

I endorse an in-your-face approach to fixing these problems. I cannot apologize for this tack in child rearing because I've met too many winners who were raised by confident parents unwilling to give in to poor and negative attitudes.

I say this because some people may be uncomfortable intruding into their sons' lives by the forceful means I've suggested. If you feel this way, consider the alternative (watching helplessly on the sidelines), and decide for yourself what to do with this information. Love your boy enough to be willing to do anything but let him rot in a swamp of negative attitudes.

Some Suggestions of Attitudes to Develop

You can build in any attitude you can think of by using these tools. You may not even know the variety of attitudes you can mold! This list will help you think of some that you might not have considered. Here are attitudes of taking initiative:

- Looking for opportunities and seizing them
- Assuming responsibility for getting things done
- Assuming blame if you're wrong
- Looking at the big picture of life
- Having determination in the face of adversity
- Being happy and maintaining a happy outlook
- Expecting good things
- Being able to handle problems
- Being friendly to people and winning others' cooperation
- Helping others
- Being able to create new attitudes
- Anticipating problems before they arise

ACTION TO TAKE

You can help your son have any attitude. This chapter provides some handles with which to grasp this cumbersome quality and helps you feel some control over what can happen. Within twenty-four hours of this moment, you will have the chance to apply something in this chapter. Enjoy your feeling of capability.

CHAPTER 13

Play Ball!

Good mental health is the ability to work and play.

—Sigmund Freud

Do what you can, with what you have, where you are.

—Theodore Roosevelt

To do what others cannot do is talent. To do what talent cannot do is genius.

—Will Henry

There are several good reasons for boys to participate in sports. Contrary to popular opinion, without good coaching the great lessons of sporting
competition will be missed. You are the coach.

BOYS ARE NATURAL GAMESMEN

I was visiting a local school for the purpose of consulting with some
teachers. As I entered the schoolyard, I saw a large group of boys playing what looked to be a combination of kick-ball and rugby. The child
at home plate would run up and boot the ball. En masse the boys
would run and attack the poor kid on the receiving end. They would

pummel him and pile on, some laughing, some squeaking, and some howling in pain.

I have a sixth sense about situations that cause litigation. That was one. I walked over and said, "What are you guys doing?" A kid who looked like Macaulay Culkin (of *Home Alone* fame) sat up and looked at me. His glasses were all bent up, and birds and stars were flying around his head.

"We're bonding, man," he said.

Recess is every kid's favorite class. The playground is the place of your first organized team game. The scene of your first fight. A place to make friends that last forever. A place to be a hero and a star. Monkey bars to climb, balls to kick, ropes to jump, races to win. It represents everything youthful and vital.

Boys are natural gamesmen. They are in constant motion: running, jumping, throwing, catching, pushing and attacking, and challenging. All these seem to be a natural part of growing up and appear in cultures worldwide.

Other factors are natural for boys too. Boys naturally clump up and form teams. Boys naturally think in terms of win-lose, who's best and who's not. They are hyperconscious of each other's athletic skill levels, and they openly challenge each other for supremacy. From the time they can walk, they actively and creatively form games and challenges to themselves.

Athletic skill is allocated to boys in differing amounts. There are about as many wonder boys as there are Humpty Dumptys. Most boys fit into the average category and have a generally high aptitude for quickly learning the tricks and skills of games. I'd like to focus this discussion on developing the talent of average boys. High and low sports performers will be discussed in the next chapter.

As a professional sports consultant, I've had the privilege of helping good athletes become great athletes. I'm in a perfect position to tell you that childhood is the cradle of champions. It is where the mind-set and the basic skills of winning are seeded. Winners aren't born; they are raised.

WHY DO BOYS LIKE GAMES SO MUCH?

There are two primary reasons. First, boys love spending energy. Playing is an economy where the currency is energy. Youthful energy is like money; the more they spend, the happier they are. What is the first thing boys do when they are set free to go out on a playground? Well, the first thing they do is run. Then they pick teams.

Which leads us to the second reason boys love games. Competition is fun and stimulating, and getting into teams has an excitement all its own. Testing himself against other boys with the hope of victory makes competing irresistible. When this excitement mixes with the naturally accelerated metabolism inside tough bodies, it's easy to understand why most boys love competition with one another. And even if your boy doesn't like to compete athletically, he shares a fiber with other boys of desiring to know how he compares.

Let's get something straight about the word *competition*. That is an adult word used to describe an adult thing. Boys *play*. I was supervising a group of about thirty boys recently at a playground. They were really roughhousing, shoving and kicking constantly. I just love moments like that because social mechanics are easy to see. I was most impressed with how *competitive* they all were.

Competitive?

NO! NO! NO! They weren't being competitive. They are boys, and they were playing. Early play sets the groundwork for adult-style competition, but boys experience a more innocent and joyous version. Teaming is fun too. This form of sociability is the easiest a child can experience because everyone has a part to play on a team and very little verbal or intellectual skill is needed. Try to keep your thinking oriented that way.

SPORTS CAN BE EDUCATIONAL

There is much more to life than winning games. If winning is only for the temporary thrill of victory, so what? I love sports and I love to win, but if sports aren't at least fun or useful in life, it's pointless participating in them. Well, sports and games are fun and useful. If you suddenly discovered that a certain sport, say, football, could teach your boy all the most critical life lessons in one season, would you sign him up? You might if the life lessons were good enough.

What life lessons? Playing hard in the face of obstacles, persevering, building stamina against the opposition, following rules, and that kind of thing. These are good lessons that can be taught in sports. But oftentimes the lessons are missed.

My folks thought little Billy could benefit from organized football. I grew up in the Lombardi era, and they thought that sacrificing my body to the gridiron gods was wholesome. I always loved sandlot football, but the mayhem characteristic of organized football left me wondering what it was all about! I remember many painful moments wondering what I did to deserve the game and why in the world I was playing it. That's where my football education failed.

It's no wonder so many parents question the importance of sports. We are a mindlessly sports-crazy country. Sports are big business, and the original intent has been drowned in a sea of glitz. Moreover, on the kids' level, too often, sports are an ego catapult for parents. Junior is forced at emotional gunpoint to play out Dad's fantasies. Too many boys are taught winning for the shallow purpose of their parents' fulfillment and entertainment.

The summer of '92 was a hot one in Denver. They had to shut

down the Little League in that city because of fighting and bickering parents. I don't know the inside story, but I can assure you that in city after city across this nation, parents pressure and harangue coaches and children to a boiling point. Don't be too shocked by this example, though; this sort of thing happens every year and has been going on for a long time. I have attended Little League games that came frightfully close to fistfights among parents. It is the darker side of parental nature—one that needs to be controlled.

We must ask ourselves, Whose life is this anyway? Could sports be of more value to our kids than simply feeling victory? Yes, of course. And the benefits of learning to do something meaningful with sports make winning all the more sweet!

If you think sports aren't worth much, it's probably because you never realized any *crossover*. Crossover means you take an experience in one realm of life and apply it to a completely different realm. Crossover is a superb reason for our kids to be involved in sports because it can teach critical life lessons such as confidence, resilience, hustle, and fair play.

Let me give you a specific example. You're at work, and the boss gives you a project that is due in an impossibly short time frame. You reluctantly accept the task, knowing you have no other option. It reminds you of that time you were at match point, down 6 games to 0 in the final set. Your opponent was serving cannonballs, and you had been having difficulty returning his serves all day. Somehow, some way you made a decision to take each shot, one at a time, and not think about anything else in the world. Concentrate on each shot, one at a time.

Here comes the serve. BOOM! You get it this time and send a perfect passing shot to the deep corner. Shot-by-shot you work your way back into the match and finally win an amazing come-from-behind victory!

Consciously or unconsciously, crossover happens when you think of that moment and decide to attack the task at hand using that athletic lesson. The lesson on the tennis court becomes tangibly valuable to improve your performance in real life. You start to work on your boss's project, one page at a time.

Making Crossover Happen

Most coaches and parents trust that participation alone in sports is enough to teach life's lessons. Nothing is that easy! Crossover fails to happen consistently for three reasons:

1. Boys just play games; they don't think about them.

2. Boys don't know the lessons to be learned, and nobody is telling them.

3. Parents don't show their sons how to apply the experiences.

Boys are just playing games. It's your job to alert your son to the valuable lessons within his game. Whether it is a sandlot baseball game or a major golf championship, teach your son to learn something new each time he plays. He probably won't always do that, but if you don't tell him, he never will.

In the summer, we used to set up a golf course around our yard. It was quite an original version with soup cans for cups and little plastic flags for pins. The kids used Nerf golf balls that went a long way. Every round was an adventure, and one never knew what sort of hazard awaited the next shot.

Golf, as you may know, is a one-of-a-kind sport, difficult to master, especially for children. The problem is, they won't admit it. I've warned mine many times that they are not ready to use real golf balls in the yard.

They didn't really understand why until one of the younger kids got one of *my* good Pinnacle balls dinged off his forehead. It was powwow time with the club pro, and the lesson was about unintended dimples and creases in skulls. After I got the disconsolate little victim settled down, we had a talk. It was not about obedience (although I mentioned it) but about what happens when you do things you are improperly prepared for. I made them all look at and touch the wound—a very compelling and fair example.

Act as though learning from sports and games is normal. Show him where to apply the lessons. Schoolwork, family problems, bullies, chores—the places you can apply the universal lesson are all around him. Expend some effort with him to locate the places where something already learned is useful. Helping your son remember and use something he already knows is the literal heart of the crossover phenomenon.

RENAISSANCE LESSONS

I've mentioned that sports and games teach lessons. What are they? The following lessons outline the base elements of Renaissance thinking and behaving. Much of this book shows applications of these skills in other contexts, but sports add a unique twist. Sports teach these traits with strange authority.

Get Your Boy in the Game

Sports lessons require direct exposure. That's all. Your boy needn't be MVP material to get in the game. Forget how much talent he does or doesn't have. Just get him in the game.

This teaches the first Renaissance lesson. It has to do with handling intimidation. Some boys are natural gamesmen; shyness and aversion to direct competition disappear with participation. Lean on your boy to mix it up with others. If he refuses, gently nudge him out for his own good. Don't let his fear stand in the way of your encouraging one of life's greatest educations!

If there is anywhere your son's genetic differences from you display themselves, it's right here. Your son may be different from you in terms of aggressiveness, physical toughness and coordination, introversion or extroversion, and so on. Remember, he's his own person. Try to disengage your emotional investment in him, and deal with him as he is.

Use Others to Help You Improve

This lies at the heart of what sports are about. How do you really know if you are doing or being your very best?

Many parents intentionally seek better competition for their sons. This search is based on an accurate notion that better competition brings out better performance from their sons. It's true. In sports, academics, or any other endeavor, boys are spurred to either improve or dissolve away in defeat in a situation where someone better is competing.

You don't want your son to dissolve. Direct competition challenges boys, and that's the reason many shy away. It's scary, and they wonder what will happen if they fail. They may not know how to compete at all, so they quit. You can help your boy by arranging competitive situations you feel he has a reasonable chance of winning *if he stretches.*

Learn the Rules, Apply Them Diligently, Anticipate, and Be Resourceful

This is a full plate of great lessons.

Diligence means following the rules, playing fair, and playing hard. Make your boy learn some basic skills of his sport, and make him practice the basics. Most boys, for example, could be much better basketball players if they would quit doing Michael Jordanesque tricks and would work on something like dribbling left-handed.

As you encourage him to master the basics of his game, remember that he isn't a pro who can automatically do whatever you tell him. Your patience and persistence are keys to teaching your son good fundamentals.

Fairness with rules is easy to teach because boys are self-policing. Cheaters get fleshed out quickly and dealt with accordingly.

Anticipation is a useful trick learned after familiarity with the rules and experience. The greatest sportsmen of our time aren't the greatest athletes but the best anticipators. Shaquille O'Neal and Kurt Warner are two excellent examples. Both players, one in basketball and the other in football, are not the most physically gifted players, but they do have a keen intuition about where the action of their game is going.

Tell your son to think ahead and plan and see what is happening next. Instruct him to feel the ebb and flow of the game and to position himself to be where the action is *going to be.* He may not understand it when you explain it, but telling him prepares him for those serendipitous moments when he realizes that it works!

Resourcefulness is much like creativity. This quality allows a player to think of unique plays or movements outside the norm of what others are doing. Imaginative play has always defined excellence in sports and, like anticipation, can be built if you coach your son to look for opportunities to do something imaginative.

Hustle and Be Aggressive

Though boys are born with doses of hustle and aggressiveness, they need development. All boys give some effort but need to be coached to give more because it's unnatural for them to move out of their comfort zone. Vince Lombardi said, "Fatigue makes cowards of us all . . . The harder you work, the harder it is to surrender . . . If you quit now, during these workouts, you'll quit in the middle of the season, during a game. Once you learn to quit, it becomes a habit."

To fulfill the requirements for a specific Cub Scout badge, my group had to run six hundred yards in less than two minutes and forty-five seconds. As you might imagine, they took off at a dead sprint, and they had sprinted to their deaths in about fifty yards. You've never heard more crying or bellyaching! "All right, then," I began, "we need to learn about *pacing*. The only way to lose a race is to stop putting one foot in front of the other. If you get tired, walk fast, but don't quit."

Boys don't know when it's time to get tired, nor do they know how hard they can play. A boy naturally drifts into a comfort zone and plateaus there unless you boost him up to the next level. Use your influence to find your boy's personal upper limits.

Inborn hustle can be increased with a little training. You're the trainer. Stay after your son, and don't allow him to get unnecessarily lax. Tired is fine, but lazy? No. Don't allow it; push your son firmly and gently.

Aggressiveness? It's more of an inborn trait, and it needs to be developed a bit differently. Start by understanding that there are two kinds of athletes in the world: those who want to be at the plate when the bases are loaded, and those who want someone else at the plate. Which one is your son?

If he is a natural player who is aggressive and confident enough to be the one at the plate, stand back and let him go. If not, understand that the problem usually is not lack of aggressiveness but lack of confidence. Confidence builds with small, successful steps of exposure to "at-the-plate" situations.

It is especially important here to apply your understanding of the differences between younger and older boys. Prior to the age of eight, try to avoid situations where hitting home runs is important. Allow your son the joy of being able to play without added worry that messing up will be "bad." Remember that at this age, boys cannot distinguish bad performance from being a bad boy. Slowly expose him to pressure moments, and do your best to make them successful. He will not win all his pressure moments, but you can help him place it all in the proper perspective by reducing the significance of his performance and highlighting the fun.

Handle Pressure

I'm frequently asked about the pressure problem of kids' sports. I'm going to give you a simple answer. Unfortunately, boys get slam-dunked into legitimate high-pressure situations too early, causing bad reactions and well-justified concern among parents. These influences require a down-to-earth and forthright action from you.

Pressure is inherent in everything we do. That pressure can be good or bad, depending on the source. There are two sources of pressure in sporting events: you and the game. The pressures of the game are good and normal and something all boys need to face. The pressures from you, however, are different and should be treated delicately. You might be a performance-oriented parent who wants your son to win everything, or you might simply value and enjoy his participation and fun. Either way, by virtue of your position as parent, you bring expectations that your boy senses. Those expectations create a type of performance pressure that can be either helpful or detrimental.

Follow some simple suggestions. Liberally apply patience and confidence to yourself. Make yourself be patient with your son. He will perform much better if he knows he can count on you to calmly support him, quietly encourage his participation, and slowly help him build his skill.

Your unswerving belief in your son is a vital force. No matter what that kid does, no matter how he plays, you must tell him that you believe in *him* (not his athletics) and believe he's the greatest person you have ever seen and he can get even better!

Handle Pain, Bumps, Bruises, and Blood, and Keep Playing

This is real-life stuff! Blood and pain are a part of life, and sports rub boys up against the harsher side of reality. Our parental inclination is to shield our sons from this, but hard as it is, we must get out of the way and let it happen.

Sports give us a way to teach the harsher truths of life in a controlled way. Explain to your son that bumps and bruises and blood are all right; he won't die. Teach him that just because he hurts doesn't mean he stops altogether. Teach him that his body will work well even when hurt, and to a *small* extent, he should press himself.

A few years ago, our younger son, Zac, got slashed by a hockey stick while he was playing in the front yard. He came in crying, looking for help. I was inside, trying to find his pet hamster that had escaped from its cage. As he was crying in the doorway about his fearful pain, I yelled to him to stop and help me find the renegade pet. The crying stopped immediately, and he got a mad, fatherly looking "where did that confounded little beast go?" glint in his eye. The tears were instantly gone, and the hunt was on!

Pain is a relative experience, no?

Don't lose your head when your son gets hurt. He takes many cues about how he should respond to all situations from you. If you freak out at the sight of blood and the possibility of pain, you can bet your boots he will, too. Pain is just pain; blood is just blood. Show him this truth.

Deal with the Pain of a Loss

This is another kind of education you must encourage. *The pain of losing is essential for winning.* Roger Staubach says in *The Name of the Game Is Life,* "If you don't hurt [over a loss], you are not going to be as competitive as you have to be to win consistently. What you don't want to do is feel so guilty [about losing] that your personality changes and you can't function."

Take note of Ralph Waldo Emerson on losing: "The indignation which arms itself with secret forces does not awaken until we are pricked and stung and sorely assailed." Emerson knew something about what a loss could accomplish: "Whilst he sits on the cushion of advantages, he goes to sleep. When he is pushed, tormented, defeated, he has a chance to learn something; he has been put on his wits, his manhood."

Losers are the ones with real opportunity in a sport match. They have the imperative to look at what they did and improve. If they handle a loss this way, they can look at themselves in the mirror and know they did their best but lost. They are the real winners. Winners gloating over victory are losing. Only those who continually improve, win or lose, are fit to wear the garland of the champion.

The problem for you will be communicating this to your son after a defeat! In an older boy, the only pain I suggest encouraging is the pain of not having done his best. The pain of a loss in a kid is usually a dead-end pain; it hurts and doesn't move anywhere. Move your kid off that pain and toward a focus of what he could have done better. List two or three things. All conversations about the loss should include the presentation of the list as the new focus of new action.

Maintain Morale and Exhibit Leadership

At this stage in the book, you understand my keen curiosity about the tick-tick-tick of interpersonal relationships. The morale of a group of interpersonal relationships called a team is remarkably complex. The more complex, the greater the opportunity for influence.

Teach your son to feel the morale of his team and do something about it. The truth of team relationships is that anyone can push the team to better performance. The problem is getting kids to believe it and then act. Your boy can be the source, and he can make his leadership felt in a variety of ways, from vocal leadership to the encouragement of total confidence in others.

General William Sherman observed of General U. S. Grant that he was ordinary in intelligence and wit, but what set him apart and made him a great leader was his "absolute belief in success." This "belief" is a very strange force that I do not pretend to fully understand. I marvel at its power to transform the ordinary into the extraordinary. You don't have to understand its strength to enjoy its rewards. Teach your son to have "absolute belief in success." That's leadership.

I heard General H. Norman Schwarzkopf quoted as saying that leadership is simple: "Take charge and do the right thing!"

If you want your son to be a leader, treat him like one. Though your son may not be what you think is a natural leader, he has the capacity to believe in himself, feel capable, and tell others to feel the same way. The leader of a group is not the person who bears the standard; the leader is the person who can get his comrades to perform. Remind your son to infect the thinking of his friends and teammates.

The Game Isn't Over

The game is never over, and that is the crux of teaching your son to come back. Kids and adults tend to look at a sporting event as a single win-lose proposition. I've found it more useful to view a sporting event from the big-picture perspective. A game is not nine innings; it's fifteen games, it's four years of high school, or it's a life.

If you bequeath this truth to your son, you will give him a priceless gem of wisdom. Our culture values a comeback kid. My kids understand that the game is never over, and they can always come back to win, even if it's the next time. I love to see that kind of fire burning in their hearts. Teach your boy this: The game is lost only when he quits. The game is in his head, not on the field. A boy who can win in his head can win on any field life presents.

ACTION TO TAKE

Just get your son in the game—any game will do. The lessons proceed once the student jumps in and plays and has you to help interpret what it all means.

CHAPTER 14

Life at the Athletic Extremes

 If your son is a superjock or a nonathlete, you may have more lessons to learn than other parents. Here is some helpful advice.

IT'S NOT JUST ABOUT SKILL

For whatever reason, you may feel as though the treatment in the last chapter is *not* relevant for you or your son. Perhaps your boy is a legitimate athletic prodigy, and you have taken unusual steps to develop his athleticism. Any discussion of sports may, you feel, be below the skyrocketing talent and potential of your boy. If that is your situation, I wish you well.

Or maybe your boy possesses little or no athletic skill. As much as you might wish or dream, the kid hasn't got it. To add insult to injury, our sports crazy world might have driven your son to feel inadequate about his lack of talent, thereby making sports participation a hated struggle.

I'd like to make suggestions to parents of athletically gifted boys and those of athletically deprived boys. I feel compelled to reiterate that sports have less to do with athletics than with achievement. Athletics is another way to push yourself to be your best. It may not even be the *best* way to achieve excellence; it's just one of the ways. This perspective has heavy implications for parents of great athletes or nonathletes.

"MY BOY IS TOO GOOD"

True athletic genius, like other aspects of genius, is present at birth. We used to live next to a kid who was riding a bike when he was two years old! When he was three, we played tag, and I couldn't catch him. He would run around like a squirrel and climb trees to escape. All the parents in the neighborhood looked at the gifted hurricane of energy, then looked at their own children and wondered what they did wrong! Parents of such boys typically show amazement at their sons' physical ability and gifts, and they are often confused about how to handle them.

Unlike other fields of genius, an athlete doesn't begin to separate from the pack until the middle of the boy phase (ages eight through ten). Up until that time, he's head and shoulders above the rest athletically, but real active talent needs physical maturity to support ability. This is also the time that a child prodigy begins to settle on a sport or physical activity in which he will make his mark.

After working with many of these prodigies, I have five suggestions you should consider. *First,* keep a close eye on the pressure you apply. Like stress, there is a fine line separating pressure that is helpful from pressure that is harmful. Throughout the boy phase, the pressure you apply should be focused more on developing skills than on winning. There is plenty of time to win but not much time to prepare the skills required for winning.

Second, find a good coach for him. Boys simply respond better athletically to good coaches than to parents. I realize that if your son wants to pursue an unusual sport like figure skating or gymnastics, you might feel the need to send him hours away to the best coach. Do that if you like, but any reputable coach stressing basics will suffice at this age level. Whatever your son likes to do athletically, put him with someone possessing specialized knowledge. That person can push your son's talent past the point you can.

Third, teach him that there is more to life than winning (beating boys of clearly lesser talent). Athletic prodigies win all the time and rarely have had the experience of losing. Winning all the time changes the lessons of head-to-head competition from "being your best" to "drubbing the opponent." This isn't good. Improving and achieving should be the focus, not simply besting an opponent.

I heard a touching story about the Special Olympics, the Olympics for children with handicapping conditions. The hundred-yard dash was hyped as the big event for the day. All the participants were waiting anxiously for the start. The official's gun went off, and the crowd rose to their feet to see a smooth, fast beginning. All the racers were moving along rapidly when a competitor in the center lane twisted his ankle and fell down on the track, squealing in pain.

The usual thing did not happen. One by one, the other competitors slowed down to look back at what had happened. Eventually, they all stopped running. In a most uncompetitive gesture, all the racers came to the aid of their stricken friend, helped him to his feet, and carried him forward across the finish line! Those boys were all winners!

Fourth, help your son become well rounded. I've worked with many talented kids for whom I've felt very sorry. No social time, no opportunity to expand horizons, no real variety in life to speak of. Many of these athletic prodigies end up pitifully naive about anything other than their sport. I don't like to see this happen. Don't let this happen to your boy. No matter how talented he may be, give him some room to vary himself. Renaissance men are bred over time to be balanced.

Fifth, teach your son to appreciate his natural gifts and help those who are less fortunate. Natural genius of any sort is a gift, one not to be taken lightly. Keep your son humble on this point, for he did nothing to earn his great skill. If he aspires to achieve great things with his talent, then he becomes something special. Encourage him to have some depth to his character by helping others so that they, too, can become better. Outside the entertainment value of exhibiting the skill and grace of an athletic genius, it's the only way I know that an athlete can give back a little of what he's been given.

"MY BOY IS NO ATHLETE"

Parents of nonathletes have what may appear to be a grim job. It seems as though these days, your son is dubbed an athletic geek if he cannot perform in one of the "Big Four" sports (football, basketball, baseball, or soccer). All boys pigeonholed in this fashion are painfully aware of their inadequacy. They are reminded constantly by the taunting of other boys, getting picked last for schoolyard games and in gym class where they know they are complete misfits. In the sporting arena, there are few places for the talentless to hide.

Consider these suggestions. *First,* with the expectation of boys with physical disabilities, very few boys have zero athletic talent. Of the hundreds of organized sports in the world, there is at least one where your son could feel the joy of getting good and being competitive with others. Think of the unusual: swimming, track-and-field events, or scuba diving. Please don't regard your son as athletically hopeless until you have explored a breadth of new options for physical competition.

Second, just as physical maturity enables athletic genius to fully display itself, physical maturity delivers hope to the talentless. Although your son may lack any hint of skill today, in six months he might become more skilled with hand-eye coordination, have improved balance, gain quickness and agility, and so on.

As a boys' coach in many sports, I've witnessed terrific performance improvement from year to year for no reason other than physical maturity. One seven-year-old kid stands out in my mind because he was so skinny. The bat he was trying to swing was bigger around than his arms! His first year was dismal because he lacked coordination of those long toothpicks. Would time help?

Yes. The next year he returned, toothpicks and all. But that year, the skinny arms that betrayed him previously were coordinated. He could crack the ball effectively, though his arms were still wiry and impotent-looking. He was able to play perfectly well, though stature- and strength-wise he hadn't really changed at all.

The rate at which boys mature physically varies widely, as do the skills that accompany the changes. That should be a great relief to you and your boy. Time can work a strange magic for your son, and he may suddenly become athletically competent.

Third, you will likely need to deal with the emotional consequences of peer mistreatment. Being ostracized by peers due to lack of athletic ability is agony for a kid. School gym classes attempt to reduce the chance of this by blending boys and girls and requiring only simple athletic chores. Still, your son may have defeating experiences and feel very bad.

Athletic play is an important social ritual for boys, so help your son find other ways to fit in. Being unable to participate in a specific sport or game is not the kiss of death. Like dealing with a boy having physical disability, you must encourage him to be as active as he is able and not to judge personal worth on the number of runs scored, baskets made, or goals saved.

It will take prolonged effort, but reassuring words from you are, as Solomon says, "like apples of gold in settings of silver." Think hard and find qualities about your son that you can honestly say are wonderful! Go the extra mile to really pump him up. He's worth it.

Paint pictures of encouragement for your son. They can come to life in his mind and be real enough for him to find solace and the will to keep trying.

Fourth, if all else fails, forget sports! It would be best if your son could be involved in some sport, but if that is not realistic, find another arena in which to stress achievement. That's the goal anyway.

This may in all candor leave you feeling disappointed, especially if you're a sports nut. You might have had fantasies of your son playing toward some wonderful athletic achievement like a Heisman Trophy or an NBA Championship. Those images might need to be shelved. Offset athletic disappointment and frustration in your son by helping him select another area in which to excel.

Fifth, encourage your son to be vigorous. I have found that what makes a difference in making a good fit socially is not so much athletic talent but the extent to which your son can be excited and vigorous. That lies not in a physical dimension but in an attitudinal dimension. Help your son thrive in any arena he finds himself, irrespective of how well he thinks he can do. Being excited and vigorous is the prime key to helping nonathletic boys succeed and fit into a world heavily biased toward the athletic elite.

KINDLING VICTORY FIRES

James Michener in his fascinating book *Sports in America* tells this story of his championship childhood baseball team: "And yet, in our little world, we were champions, and from that simple fact radiated an inner confidence that has never left me. I could never become a bum, because I was a champion."

Do your boy a favor, and expect success from him. Expect success in anything he tries. Expect victory in a matter-of-fact way, and your son will get adjusted to thinking that winning is normal. He will get accustomed to it, and with some kindling from you, he will start a victory fire in his heart that will not be extinguished by any defeat.

Let him win games on occasion so that he can feel the sensation of winning. Look for and arrange victory situations for him as often as possible. Be on the constant lookout for situations you can arrange to be surefire wins for your kid. Avoid, if you can, situations that are sure-fire losses.

Additionally, remember that parents and children are not playing the same game, though it may look that way. At one Little League game, it struck me that all the parents in the stands were watching a different game. Inside each skull was a game going on where the son was the center of action. The game going on in the field bore no like-ness to the ones going on in the heads of the parents.

In a similar vein, be aware that the game you want your son to play and the one he is playing are different. I've found it useful in our quiet moments to explore what my son is playing for and to encourage suc-cess and victory in ways important to him. That kind of coaching will be soundly effective and appropriate.

ACTION TO TAKE Do your part to actively help your son in sports. Create an agenda with your boy, and play for the sheer delight of playing.

CHAPTER 15

Mastery: A Better Way for Boys to Feel Good About Themselves

Let's go back to the drawing board and rethink the topic of self-esteem. A boy equipped with mastery really has something to talk about!

I LOVE PEOPLE AROUND ME WHO THINK THEY CAN DO THE IMPOSSIBLE

All the great leaders in history have had an odd quality: They didn't find success; they created it. Like any vast source of energy, they spun off action and dynamism in such quantity that the world changed in response to their efforts. They had an ability to make things happen through the power of conviction and belief.

I know a half dozen people like this. They are very unusual and exciting. They fill my waiting sails with confidence and somehow radiate enough enthusiasm about "the possible" to sweep me and others along! Their energy seems to have a vacuuming, updraft effect. I love having them around me because I know they're tapped into an energy that makes progress happen. It's very catching, and I love the feeling.

I've studied this driving energy and the people who create it. Most of the people I've interviewed chuckle because they don't know what "it" is, either! They just do it.

What is this creative, motivational energy? Perhaps it's the manifestation of crystal-clear direction combined with bullheadedness. Perhaps it's the high-temperature confidence focused on people and events. Could it be steely determination mixed with generous doses of quiet and unshakable belief? They seem to know that they can handle any eventuality, and they have enough faith in their resourcefulness to try anything.

What they have is pure Renaissance. Though I've chased many shadows in this search, I've concluded that this energy has distinctions and is traceable and teachable. The way this energy enables the possessor to seemingly breeze through obstacles is a source of inspiration for those of us who struggle through each day.

TALK IS CHEAP

Boys are notoriously big talkers. I wish I had a dime for every time I've heard some boy in my life brag about some possession or talent or experience! I find it hard to believe that a number of kids in my neighborhood have practiced with the Detroit Tigers, climbed Mount Everest, and driven their mom's car. One fellow told me not long ago that he once water-skied one hundred miles per hour!

Talk is cheap. I've made studied observations of boys who brag a lot. They may look and act like those at the top, but they talk and trudge around in hopeless circles. They have lots of great ideas and terrific potential but not the slightest awareness of the success energy *they* must generate to move ahead. The world races past as they talk and talk.

Nobody wants his boy to grow up to be a cheap dreamer or a senseless talker. Somehow, some way you want to give your son the key to action, the power to move rather than just talk. You want him to be a Renaissance man. That's a noble urge, full of virtue and possibility. Start to want it more because you can help create it.

What Is the Difference Between a Resourceful Doer and a Talker?

If you are like many other parents, you have an intuitive sense that getting your boy to be a person of action now means he won't be a big talker later. He won't have to be! He'll understand accomplishment, and he'll appreciate the difference between knowing how to do something and doing it.

I grew up by a kid who had more Boy Scout merit badges than anybody else in the country. He was *the* legitimate national champion. Let me ask you: Was he a talker or a doer? He was draped with awards—pins, medallions, sashes, patches, and ribbons. He was a spectacle! And he was smart; he could do almost anything. What really set him apart was that he was willing to do almost anything.

The difference is critical. Many boys know how to do things, but for whatever reason, they shy away from the prospect of pressing forward with goals and accomplishments. Others, though not always knowing what to do, are willing to jump forward and make things happen.

Twenty-first-century Renaissance men will learn and practice the fearlessness of the latter group. They will be lifted out of mediocrity by the parents who appreciate the dangers of the jungle in which we live, the parents whose entire focus is on making sons capable jungle fighters. How shall we lift our sons out of mediocrity and teach them to run with the big wolves? Don't say self-esteem or I'll scream!

SELF-ESTEEM HAS RUN OUT OF STEAM

Self-esteem is unfortunately becoming a shopworn echo in our lives. I feel a strong urge to share my discontent with this term. For like so many before it, it has gained a life of its own and its meaning has drifted far from the original. The fundamental concept is still good, but the common meaning is exhausted.

Colloquially, it's understood as feeling good about yourself. Self-esteem was labeled in the fifties and sixties by Dr. Norman Vincent Peale as feeling good about yourself based on accomplishments and skills learned on the road to excellence. It means something different today.

Now, building self-esteem through positive "self-talk," incessant praise and reward, rates as the psychological fix of choice for a wide array of behavioral dysfunctions! Here are examples of self-talk:

- "I'm a good and deserving person."

- "I'm a winner."

- "I'm competent and growing stronger daily."

- "I'm a good student and deserve the best."

There is nothing wrong with saying positive things to yourself. But this constant self-praise has become epidemically foolish. We're encouraged to dole out praise to ourselves and our children without plan or justification. It's like emotional welfare: If you breathe, you deserve to be told you're wonderful. Our society has thrown around this self-praise stuff so often that it no longer means anything. It's no wonder people aren't tangibly improving. The incessant positive self-talk is vacuous and valueless!

Fact is, we all know deep down that we're not so great and that excellence must be achieved. This is difficult to admit. We are notoriously prone to believe information that supports our most cherished hopes about ourselves, even when that information is idiotic or wrong. The popular mental health doctrine holds that feeling good about yourself is the same as being good. This is an unfortunate ruse that only postpones the bitter truth that excellence must be earned.

I ran into this constantly in my practice. It often seemed contradictory to me that so many people would seek out my advice after hours of positive ego propping. If self-talk worked so well, why were so many braggart boys so goofed up? Self-talk always proved itself empty as the sole means of getting motivated and being one's best. But many people wanted to believe that in their hearts they were good and wonderful people. The self-esteem bandwagon assured us we needn't assume responsibility for our faults. It was socially acceptable to suffer from low self-esteem.

Maybe you better sit down and open wide. This is strong medicine: You can't duck the responsibility of being your best by talking. As I look around, it seems to me that some people should feel bad about who they are. Are they doing anything of great value? Are you? Where in the world did the idea come from that people had the inalienable right to feel good about themselves? Did anyone ever hear of real accomplishment? Real talent? Does service to people or contribution to humanity matter? And this doesn't even begin to address the spiritual dimension. Find me a passage in the Bible that says you must feel good about yourself. It *does* say to forget yourself.

Self-esteem is not the point of a successful life. Self-esteem is one of the means to create a life where you can do some good for others.

WE NEED TO FIND SOMETHING THAT WORKS

When Dr. Peale first spoke of self-esteem, he didn't expect it to become our nation's religion. Let's stop patting ourselves on the back and reciting empty choruses of "How Great I Art!" We're real-world people, and we know better. Let's dismiss self-esteem; it has tried, but it hasn't moved us toward anything that produces real life. Let's change from feeling good about ourselves to being good at doing things of value.

I'll never forget one child I worked with. He had little slogans plastered across his notebook. Put there by his well-meaning parents, the "warm fuzzies" and "good vibes" messages weren't making it. The kid was a troll. I can still hear him reading aloud off his notebook all the snappy sayings about goodness and self-esteem. He'd always finish by looking up at me and giving me an "I've got this game figured out" wink. Not cute. The child remained so nasty I could hardly stand him. He made me conclude that there is an irreducible difference between saying good things to yourself and actually being good.

I spend more of my time with kids building talent and ability than telling them they are wonderful. I've discovered that kids quickly figure they are good if they can do things. Talent and accomplishment are self-rewarding, and they are more compelling than current methods of raising self-esteem.

Does such an approach have a name? We love to have titles for processes, so this one will be called *mastery.*

What Is Mastery?

The word *mastery* has been used for years to describe spending time, exerting effort, and producing proof of excellence in a fixed endeavor. That was the original intent behind the trades. A young person was accepted to study a skill such as masonry, blacksmithing, woodworking, or glassblowing with a master. The young person was an apprentice, working up to a journeyman and, eventually, after considerable time, training, and demonstration of a skill, a master.

What could a boy master? Literally anything: calligraphy, art, computers, animal husbandry, gardening, and many other talents. Some great sources of ideas for what to master are the Cub and Boy Scouts manuals, 4-H materials, youth enrichment classes at a local college, Junior Achievement groups, and hobby classes. They are filled with ideas, any one of which would be appropriate for this quest.

What does mastery produce? In addition to specific skills, it produces reasonable confidence. Reasonable confidence is having surety of self-worth based on a tangible, developed skill. Boys love doing things, and they love even more doing things well. The sense of achievement created by real skill is of a different fiber and depth than that of verbal praise. You cannot talk your son into the same level of self-confidence that's possible if he builds it for himself.

How Do You Create Mastery?

First, let your boy choose to master what he wants. His unique pool of biases and talents is huge, and he might choose things to master that leave you scratching your head! I worked with a boy who had no evidence of any interests whatever. He sat around, in my terms, "thinking zeros." A real flat-liner. His parents had creatively tried all avenues to encourage him, but nothing seemed to work. He didn't respond.

One day, to my surprise, he began talking to me about CB radios. I was amazed at how much he knew, especially since his parents were not the least bit technical. As it turned out, he would sit by his bedroom window and listen to his neighbor talk on his CB deep into the night. He'd received a real education, and nobody, least of all his neighbor the "master," knew! The little kid rattled off all sorts of stuff about CBs that I'd never heard before. You should've seen the relieved looks on Ma's and Pa's faces when informed of the discovery. I didn't see him again until after Christmas when he brought in his spanking new CB radio.

Sometimes boys don't know what they are good at, and they won't attempt to master anything. I can tell you countless other tales of helping boys discover talents inside themselves they didn't know existed. One boy with a great ear learned to imitate birdcalls, another with thin fingers became a capable guitar player, and another with great interpersonal skills I fear may have become a con man! Boys are blind to themselves. They have uniqueness that goes unnoticed unless somebody like you says something. Appreciate what it means that all boys have their own special gifts. Your job at this point is not so much to choose the things that your son will master but to highlight things in which he is precocious. Perhaps he is particularly responsible, understanding, smart, strong, vocal, creative, or funny.

Observing and mentioning obvious traits you see establishes their tangible existence in your boy's mind. You can literally open a child's eyes to what he could not see. Then he can begin to recognize the gifts upon which he should rightfully build skill and talent.

I worked with a little chap who had many strikes against him. He had a congenital cleft palate, which had been clearly difficult to repair. He had thick glasses and a perpetually runny nose. I would almost cry when he would leave my office because he tried so hard to be loved and accepted by other kids, who were merciless with him. But God bless him, he was a scrapper, and he never quit.

His handicapping condition was his greatest gift, and he didn't know it. Nobody had ever mentioned to the young boy what a natural inspiration he was to other people. He inspired me and everyone else who knew him. I told him that rather than run and hide because of his physical appearance, he should show it off and tell other people that he could rise above their dumb problems.

Always remember that your job is that of a highlighter. Your spoken observations germinate ideas in your boy's head. Don't hesitate to mention the obvious. What he chooses to master is up to him.

Nothing limits him. My very good friend and comrade in mischief is an emergency-room physician named Frank Redmond. Frank has taught me the truth that "if any man can do it, you or I could learn to do it." We go back and forth frequently discussing other jobs we would like to learn, and Frank is forever teasing my imagination by saying, "You could learn how to do that!" He taught me how to sew an aorta together over lunch one day, with the encouragement to go home and practice. I'm thankful for Frank because he constantly frees me from thinking, *I couldn't do that.*

Teach this to your son with words and with your actions. Help him explore the vast range of options he can conceive, and don't permit him to succumb to your boundaries. Help him reach the stars; put him up on your shoulders if you must. You can do that!

ACTION TO
TAKE

The best action to take at this point is to rush on to the next chapter and do a few of the activities discussed!

CHAPTER 16

Hot Tips for Creating Mastery

 Here is your practicum on mastery training. It's easier to create than you might think!

CLEVER, CLEAR WAYS TO PRODUCE MASTERY

In this chapter I want to offer you a set of conditions for mastering mastery.

Watch and listen for your chances to work these ideas. Your son will tell you the things he wishes to ace. Your job is to be the master of support and help him aim high. Help him dream *up* the ladder of achievement, not down. Allow him to set the pace, as you become his comrade in achievement. But by all means, remember . . .

IF YOU DON'T BELIEVE IN THIS BOY, YOU ARE HIS WORST ENEMY

You must be relentless in your belief in your son. He knows very well whether or not you believe in him, and if by chance he's unclear, he'll guess pessimistically. You must discipline yourself to speak forth boldly for your boy and confidently attack areas he chooses to master. Hand-wringing and second-guessing are strictly forbidden! Your son needs to understand the plain fact that no matter what, you believe that he can do anything he sets his mind to and you fully support his earnest efforts.

Brag about your boy in front of other adults. What a great reward! What a vivid message! He will hear the words that you tell another adult, and with the ears of his heart he will hear that you love him and are proud to be his parent. That alone is worth the effort to seek to brag to another person in front of him.

UNDERSTAND CRAWDAD PSYCHOLOGY

My dad used to tell me that people were like crawdads in a bucket. If one reached up and started to climb out, the others would grab him by the legs and drag him back down.

Warn your boy about the naysayers. The world seethes with nega-tivism and negative people, the handwringers and "the sky is falling" crowd. They want to steal your kid's optimism and hope. You need to teach your son to disregard people who say, "No, it can't be done that way," or "You'll never be able to do that," or worse yet, "Nobody else can do that, and you won't be able to, either." Your son needs to learn the skill of defiantly ignoring the crawdad and running the other way.

Some of them might be his best friends. The unfortunate truth is that one's crawdad friends are oftentimes the biggest impediment to success. Unless a friend has enough humility and love to help another up and out of the crawdad bucket, the person is a phony rendition of a real friend.

This is a particularly vital truth in choosing things to master. Most boys will quit trying to succeed if they don't get an immediate victory and they have to face the interminable crawdad. The more outlandish or lofty a goal, the harder those crawdads yank. I guarantee you that the minute some crawdad says, "It can't be done," somebody out there is doing it!

PREPARE TO IGNORE BAD CIRCUMSTANCES

It's possible to ignore the obstacle that life plants in your path. Some people have a capacity to act as if problems don't exist, and they plow forward. I do know that from the smallest feat to the most awesome achievement, trouble stalks you, and impediments line the route. Will your son obey them or ignore them?

How should we teach boys about these problems? Well, since negative circumstances are always going to be there, I suggest that you prepare your son in advance and let him know that trouble, discouragement, and hardship are part of winning. A boy who knows these parts of the program is not nearly so staggered as a boy who is surprised by unanticipated difficulty.

My friend Mike and I took a group of boys camping one cold fall weekend. I, being the urban, rational person that I am, wanted to sleep in the cabin. Mike, being a crazed, Daniel Boone outdoorsy type, wanted to sleep under the stars. I was the only one who wanted to sleep in the cabin. Thankfully, I had the chance to warn three of the six boys who slept outside that they would freeze, get bugs in their hair, and wake up smelling like burned logs.

Guess what happened? The three kids who were forewarned didn't have nearly the bad experience of the three who had no idea what was coming. The three who had the warning dealt with the reality of cold feet and hard ground, whereas the other three bitterly complained about their discomfort. They all experienced exactly the same things, but some had been mentally prepared and some had not.

Speak boldly to your son about real-life obstacles! Warn him! Suggest to him that he won't encounter anything not faced before by another boy. By all means, acknowledge any fears he may have, and urge him to try in spite of them. Recite the "Parent's Pledge," making public your covenant to help him get through life's problems to victory. Assure him of his talent and skill, and focus his attention on them rather than on obstacles that may (or may not) lurk in the future.

REWARD INITIATIVES WITH ATTENTION

You must sharpen yourself to notice efforts by your son to master something. Challenge yourself to notice any initiative he shows and reward it with his favorite treat—your attention! Any initiative means any action he starts by himself for the purposes of learning or doing something new. This golden break comes more often than you think.

In fact, it might come your way daily. Our kids bring home schoolwork every day and display with considerable pride all they've done. They don't do this routine for fun; they want us to be proud. I oblige that hunger by gushing all over them. Seize the brief moments without thinking; jump in and fan the fire! Take the time to show him you care.

Maybe you think you won't have the time available for this. Listen, your time is the greatest reward you can give your boy. Make time. If you haven't the luxury of much time to spare in the day, I suggest scheduling time slots to create more.

I found by accident that when I spent the whole evening with my kids, they always felt as though they didn't get enough of me. They would complain about getting cheated out of time, unfairness, and so on. I was exasperated after putting aside four to five hours to make sure that *didn't* happen.

This is what I did. I told each kid that I would spend a focused half hour alone with him or her. Nothing else would interrupt our time during that time slot, and the child would have my complete, uninterrupted attention. It was perfect. I spent about two hours total with them, and they felt as though they got more of my time than when I had committed the whole four-hour night.

HELP YOUR BOY FIND HEROES

Boys need heroes. Boys, due to the immature quality of their personalities, are constantly on the hunt for adults to emulate. That is part of how they naturally grow and develop. Your boy's choice of heroes is not always in your control, but your direction and advice are important determining factors.

Who are your boy's heroes? Probably athletes, musicians, and movie stars. A large part of advertising hype for stars is aimed at developing a heroic public image. Advertisers understand the impact of heroes, and they use that knowledge to sell more tennis shoes and sugar water. As we've watched countless public heroes stumble, it should be obvious that those we're told are heroes don't necessarily qualify.

Press the idea of selecting qualified and proven heroes with your son. Ask him some questions. Why does he like them specifically? What does he think that hero or role model could teach him if he had some time to spend with him? What valuable lessons can you as a dad learn from his heroes? What do his heroes tell you about his wishes and hopes and dreams? If his hero were in his shoes, how would he conduct himself?

Don't try to railroad him into getting new heroes. Get him to think a bit about this whole business. Keep in mind that the purpose of a hero is to set the pace for personal achievement, not to have a new idol to worship. Help your son stop worshiping and start keeping pace with the people he lionizes.

My kids love former All-pro quarterback Joe Montana. Over the years I've been able to use this adoration in a number of useful ways. They've heard me say a thousand times, "What would Joe Montana do?"

"Dad, we played hit-ball today, and I was terrible!" Jake once said.

"What are you gonna do about it, Joe?"

Pretty good question, eh? It's amazing what transpires with such a little tweak. He'll begin to think about what Joe Montana would do in this situation or that, and it's almost as good as having Joe there to give advice directly.

"He'd probably try to figure out what he was doing wrong, Dad."

"Oh, would you like some suggestions from me?" I'd offer.

"No, I think I know what the problems are."

Let boys have their role models, and leverage their mental presence whenever possible. You are probably the only hero your son will ever have the chance to really know.

Arrange Surefire Wins

I mentioned in chapter 14 your son's need to feel victory. You must arrange situations that are absolute, surefire wins. It is through repeated victory that he learns to expect winning. Success becomes second nature only after it's experienced firsthand a number of times.

If your son tries something, do everything in your power to let him feel victory. For example, during pickup basketball games in our neighborhood, if one of the smaller kids makes an exceptionally good play or pass, I give a little extra effort to make sure his team wins the point. That way he can feel victory and what it means to create winning.

Along with arranging victories is learning the fine art of savoring them. Have you ever watched kids replay in super slow motion a shot or a hit or a catch they made? What are they doing? They are savoring, indulging, delighting! Join them. Ask to see it again. Ask how it felt: "Did that catch win the Super Bowl?"

Once we had a junior sports competition at our church. Each child had an event in which to compete, but there was one small condition we placed on all competitors. After each event, they had to replay it all in slow motion. The slow-motion replay was much more fun than the competition, especially for the people in the audience who had to cheer in slow speed. It was a time of great savoring and, therefore, great fun.

After a victory, any victory, big or small, your son will want to discuss the details of what happened. Draw him out with enthusiasm and curiosity. Ask him to teach you how he does such wonderful things. The savory instants will burn indelible memories in your relationship together.

GET YOUR SON TO DO THE THINGS HE DOESN'T THINK HE CAN DO

Any talent consists of a combination of smaller actions that almost anyone can do. Climbing trees is grabbing one branch and pulling yourself up, then grabbing another branch and going up again. Playing viola is picking up the instrument and holding it, then putting one finger on one string and pulling the bow across that one string. Becoming a world-renowned virtuoso takes just a little more practice! Skateboarding? Find a skateboard and stand on it. Within ten minutes that will get boring, so put one foot on the ground. Within ten more minutes that will get boring, so push a little bit, and so on.

Boys have trepidation because they become intimidated by looking at an entire polished activity, for example, being at the top of a tree or playing Beethoven or skating in the national championships, and thinking, *There's no way!* You can get a boy to do almost anything if you show him that any activity is a specific, boring sequence of behaviors that he may already know how to do. Once shown that everything is, at the core, quite basic, most boys will gather the courage to try anything.

All you can do is fail, right? And what happens then? Get up and try it again.

Let me tell you another old trick: Boys will try to do things you forbid them to try. I worked a corollary of this rule with a kid who wanted to learn how to throw a Frisbee. He was a defeated soul who told me he couldn't because he didn't know how to hold it. I brought a Frisbee to one of our sessions and asked him to go outside with me to throw it. He wouldn't even pick the thing up because he said he didn't know what to do. So, I put it in his hand in a very awkward way, cocked his arm backward in a very uncomfortable position, and told him to freeze. "Don't move," I said, "and by all means don't drop the Frisbee now."

Within about thirty seconds he was very agitated about the uncomfortable situation, and he begged me to allow him to move. I said, "It's all right to move, but don't drop the Frisbee down right here," and I pointed to a spot right in front of me on the ground. He obeyed, and he threw it down on the ground five feet in front of him.

BUILD RESOURCEFULNESS

What would I wish for my son if I could teach him only one survival quality? Resourcefulness.

Having an attitude of resourcefulness gives you the best possible chance to creatively affect the world around you.

When resourcefulness meets up with a problem, it asks, "How can I fix it?"

When resourcefulness meets up with a need, it asks, "How can I fill it?"

When resourcefulness meets up with a challenge, it asks, "How can I whip it?"

When resourcefulness meets up with insurmountable odds and overwhelming adversity, it says, "There must be a way; if there is any possible way to fix this, I can find it, too. The answer won't jump into my lap, so I better find it or find someone to find it or find someone to find someone to find it."

Do you get the idea? Resourcefulness is probably best described as the inability to quit in the pursuit of what you want, to search all options and create them if necessary. It's best built with real-world problems; combined with tutoring from you. Don't permit your boy to give up on the solutions to a difficulty without exhausting all the avenues of answers.

Perhaps you've heard these comments commonly attributed to Calvin Coolidge.

Nothing in the world can take the place of persistence. Talent will not; nothing is more common than unsuccessful men with talent. Genius will not; unrewarded genius is almost a proverb. Education will not; the world is full of educated derelicts. Persistence and determination alone are omnipotent. The slogan "press on" has solved and always will solve the problems of the human race.

Teach your son to memorize the four magic words for resourcefulness: *Can you help me?*

When I tell my kids to call for pizza, they know they are not calling for pizza; they are calling for help. When the kids need to do reports for school, they go to the library for help. They don't go to the doctor for medicine; they go to the doctor for help. Do you sense the difference here? People are always willing to help others; teaching your son the ability to ask by using these words is priceless. These four words will open doors for your son like a magic key.

List resources and keep them handy: libraries, encyclopedias, well-placed people, newspapers, magazines, other parents, organizations, the government at all levels, toll-free numbers (1-800-555-1212 is the national toll-free information line), and Web sites to name a few.

If you teach your son to consider that life is at his disposal, you won't have to worry about him taking care of himself. Not only will he do that with distinction, but he will be a model and resource to others as well.

Make Good Decisions

The comedian Gallagher posed this question: "Why are there floods?" The answer is, "There are floods because water can make a decision."

If there is one skill deserving every boy's mastery, it's the skill of good decision making. Very early in my life, I was encouraged to make good decisions. Like all people, sometimes I did, and other times I didn't. But thanks to the fact that someone encouraged me, I was constantly aware of the need to make wise choices. I knew from early coaching that good decisions could get me places that bad decisions couldn't. The quality of my life would be inexorably linked to the decisions I made.

You can teach this to your boy in many ways. The most crucial skill in making prudent choices is that of evaluating possibilities and outcome. Don't take this skill lightly, for your son hasn't much of an idea how this is done. Start by teaching him the value of writing down ideas and options.

Ben Franklin relied on the method of listing "Pros" of a decision on one column of a sheet of paper and "Cons" on the opposite column. Comparing the columns of pros and cons allowed him to make a clear, rational analysis of his choices. Your son can follow a similar pattern by thinking up all the resulting scenarios rippling out from any decision he might make. Encourage him, and help him think up as many options and ripples to the options as possible. Write them down! This is very important. Look at long-term and short-term effects and unintended consequences, and create secondary plans.

Earlier, I discussed the value of TimeFraming™, and I advocate its application here. Draw in logical detail how decisions will play out over the course of two or three frames. For example, if your son needs to make a decision relating to playing soccer after school, mowing lawns, or studying more to get better grades, draw the frames, and fill in the potential positive and negative ramifications of each decision.

Above all else, make certain that your son learns the value of applying logic to decisions. Make certain that he has good, solid, and logical reasons for his choices. Get in the habit of quizzing him after he makes decisions to check and teach logic and common sense. I strongly urge you to let him cut his teeth on either a created scenario demanding a good decision or a personal decision of yours that needs to be made.

Not long ago, our station wagon was ready to die. I wanted to buy a minivan, but the prices seemed obscene. For fun, we had a family meeting in which all the options were laid out for the kids, and we heartily encouraged their input. The options included buying a new minivan, complete with costs and responsibilities, buying a used one, with all the potential liabilities, or buying a horse. For a lot of logical reasons, they voted for the horse.

Created situations and personal decisions are useful teaching tools because they are easy to evaluate and review. There is no adequate replacement for practice and rehearsal when it comes to learning to make proper decisions. Real-life examples are excellent.

Encourage your boy to make wise decisions. Wise decisions are made from the perspective of a higher calling: decisions made for the benefit of others, decisions that involve health or harm, decisions requiring moral or ethical thoughtfulness. Your son cannot make deeply wise choices at his age, but it certainly isn't too early to get him to think about the significance of wisdom.

Your son should appreciate that sometimes the wise choice is not always the easiest or most convenient option. This kind of decision making requires maturity and thoughtful encouragement from a seasoned adult. Wise choices require modeling, and you'll have to walk him through a few to show him the way.

I use the newspaper to practice this. A newspaper is nothing more than a catalog of decisions that people have made and the responses caused by the decisions. Pick one up tonight, and lay out any scenario you like for your son: "Given this and this and this, what would you do?" Follow that up with, "Well, this is what that fellow did, and look what happened." Boys love this procedure because it's real. They can look at the pictures and see the faces.

Despite your most earnest and diligent efforts, your boy will make silly and senseless choices. It's all due to youth and honest inexperience. I remember as a young boy, our home had a nice fireplace. One night I was the last one up so I thought I should put out the fire. There were two smoldering logs, and I picked them up with big log tweezers and threw them in the garbage can under a desk. I remember thinking how logical it was to throw them away; after all, isn't the garbage can where you put stuff you don't want? Soon after, I remember thinking how illogical it was that fire should be coming out from under my mom's desk!

A boy's decision making can be dangerously wrong. Teach and test; teach and test. He'll get the hang of it, but not without your guidance.

HAVE JOIE DE VIVRE

This is French for "love of life." In some respects this section should have appeared at the beginning of the book. Sensitive people recognize that many things in life hinge on one's outlook. Life is full of assets and liabilities, and the extent to which you find the good in this mysterious gift of life determines your level of enjoyment.

Actively loving your life requires practice. It is something you commit, an activity you perform. To have joie de vivre, you must be optimistic and expectant of good things in the future, and relaxed and joyous enough to see finer things in life today.

Reasonable confidence produces within your son the ability to operate effectively in life, and it allows him to make lemonade out of lemons. When it's mixed with joie de vivre, a remarkably well-blended child forms. A kid like that has a bearing that puts him above the crowd, and he is a blessing to you, your family, and everyone who meets him.

But the picture is not yet complete. If you did nothing more than what's been outlined in the book so far, you would have bequeathed to your son love and attention and skill not to be matched by any parent. But to give him all that you can possibly give, you must not forget faith.

ACTION TO TAKE

This chapter is full of activities. Don't try to do them all quickly; that will only frustrate you and your son. Take your time and enjoy them.

CHAPTER 17

The Ultimate Challenge

Science and technology are climbing the mountain of mystery, and they will find when they arrive at the top that faith was waiting the whole time.

—*Peter O'Toole in the movie* Creator

As I look back on my life, I see that I was constantly brought to a crossroads which demanded a choice which way I should go. I believe that the key to my success is that I seemed to have consistently chosen the least traveled path.

—*George Mueller*

This book is full of important, challenging ideas. Each has its place in the big picture. But the following challenge is most important of all. Read and carefully consider what you must do.

I MUST CHALLENGE YOU ONE FINAL TIME

Writing this chapter has been very difficult for me. The writing itself has been easy. The trouble has been trying to make sure there will be no misinterpretation. Misinterpretation, as you will recall, is normal in human discourse. But misunderstanding what I'm saying here could have devastating consequences for you and your son. That worries me.

It's a strange paradox with only one solution: Say it, and let the chips fall where they may. Please read carefully.

The Renaissance road is certainly not for the fainthearted. Those of us committed to making a generation of extraordinary men understand the obstacles facing us. In response, we have made sober, wise choices to prepare for the job. In this book, I have done my level best to provide tools to make the task winnable. My deepest hope is that you will find courage and resolve in these pages, and that you will use these tools to build a unique boyhood for your son.

I would be defeating my efforts if I didn't share one final ingredient. If you applied all the information in these pages, you would become remarkably effective in raising your boy. But you also would be going off into the cruel world half-cocked. There's no reason to do that. There is another side to boy rearing that's about as unconventional and critical as anything we've covered. There is good reason to carefully consider the following words and accept what I think is your ultimate challenge.

THE FOUR PILLARS OF LIFE

I've considered several people in my life my mentors. One in particular had some unorthodox perspectives on life, but he made me think.

His thought life rested on four pillars: work, play, the arts, and mystery. This is an interesting thought that helped focus this book. We've examined how to construct the first three pillars: I've talked about how to work with your boy, how to play with him, and how to expand his creativity. Mystery, however, is the area I've saved till last.

Many endeavors of humanity have been aimed at trying to pierce this ever-present shroud of mystery in life. Science attempts to do it with a rigid method of experimentation. Mathematics does it with a meticulous conceptual system of postulates and proof. Philosophers make their efforts using the brilliant invention called logic. The poets find meaning and understanding following their unique paths. In their own way, they are attempting to make sense out of life. Nobody has completely succeeded.

There's always more to uncover. We seem hounded by this urge to find more. One would almost think that we are destined, driven perhaps, to find higher truths. We act as though we're hungry for something. There is only one universal in our collective attempts to make sense of the mystery: Everyone must take a step of faith. Everyone. Faith permits us to move forward despite unknowns. Faith is the solitary bridge through the swirling fog of mystery. The quality of your future depends on the quality of your faith.

LET ME INTRODUCE YOU TO THE LIVING BRIDGE

We all must put our faith into something. In the U.S., ordinary faith surrounds us. In this age of family values, having religion in our lives has great curb appeal. Institutional Christianity is by far the most popular source of religious fulfillment in the U.S. It's not really all that lively, and it's notoriously unfulfilling. Some of us still have faith in technology to save humankind, but I believe we are smart enough to know when we are spitting into the wind. Belief in the better nature of humankind is hot if you don't read the papers or believe music lyrics or think.

Unfortunately, all these faiths fail. The world is standing around with two torn-off bootstraps hanging from its fingers. We pulled too hard. Now, what do we do?

There is nothing ordinary or popular about what I am going to suggest. Your son is growing quickly, and you haven't the luxury of a shaky bridge of faith. I suggest a faith that is elemental Renaissance: a new birth. It is faith firm and sure and very alive. It's fit to usher your son to a spectacular life.

I come from a very specific spiritual persuasion best summed up by a Chinese professor early in the fall of 1989. That summer the terrible riots struck Beijing, and hostile political repression culminated in the deadly Tiananmen Square incident. He observed that the brutal hatred and repression proved that the human heart is evil. This is different from Eastern and Western philosophies and humanistic thinking, which hold the opposite view. He said, "The Chinese are following *Jesus* in droves because He is the only 'religion' that has a realistic worldview."

Jesus stands out in history. We still grapple with the provocative nature of His words and deeds. He made prophecies that came true. His wisdom was unconventional in every way. He demonstrated miraculous power. If all that wasn't enough, He rose from the dead, fulfilling a prophecy He made about Himself. Perhaps this is a person we should take more seriously!

Consider, for instance, some of His odd wisdom.

- He said that a man's life is no better than the foundation upon which it's built.

- He said that people are unclean not because of what goes into them, but because of what comes out of them.

- Jesus said that to enter the kingdom of heaven, you have to be born again.

- He told us to come boldly before God with our request.

- He said men's hearts are dark but fixable.

- He said to forgive one another.

- He compared the kingdom of God to trees, children, money, and other things.

- He said forceful men were seizing the kingdom of God.

- He told us that we needed to become like children to inherit the kingdom of God.

- He preached radical selflessness.

- He offered boundless forgiveness.

- He talked about gaining treasure in heaven.

- He told us to love our enemies.

- He promised us eternal life.

- He offered us the Holy Spirit.

- He said that with the Holy Spirit upon us, we would do greater things than He did.

- He said we would have to battle a persistent attraction to evil.

- He said that a person's history has nothing to do with happiness.

- He said that if you follow Him, the world won't be happy with you.

- He said that with faith the size of a mustard seed, you can move mountains.

And He said much, much more.

THE LESS-TRAVELED PATH

If these ideas don't spark you or frustrate your mind, check your pulse! Put this book down and think about this: Jesus knows us. He speaks from a source not of this earth. And He is misunderstood.

Jesus told us to believe in Him as the bridge to a good life. He said that the conditions of a person's heart determine the quality of life. He offers us a reconditioned heart. He knew that the world would impugn every man's and woman's faith in Him and would stand squarely against Him. He was right. He has challenged us to ignore this barrier and consider Him the bridge of faith to a complete and nourishing life. This is not an oft-traveled path.

I've checked out other paths. I traveled the philosophy path in college, and I found it going in circles. I discovered that the new psychology path led into the middle of a swamp. New Age metaphysics is really a dirt trail going nowhere. I tried living a good life, but it seemed empty. I can tell you from personal experience that the path offered by Jesus is the one we, as thinking people, cannot ignore any longer. I ignored it for short periods of time in my life and I came rushing back due to starvation, confusion, and extreme restlessness.

Your life must be based on something of eternal value in order to be sensible and coordinated. The words and deeds of Jesus make sense to me, and they provide my life with value and distinction beyond anything I've seen on any other path.

I heard it said that we have more in common with Adolf Hitler than we do with Jesus! It's difficult to rise above the squalor of our dark innards. We need help and guidance now. We need a patient and forgiving Teacher now. Jesus is here, alive, and willing to help now.

The world will not like for you to be a cleansed, empowered member of the kingdom of God. That's what happens when you lift your eyes to heaven and say, "Jesus, I am Yours." I think you should do it. You don't need to become anything other than devoted follower of Jesus. He wants only one thing from you—your heartfelt devotion.

Your son should find his faith in a radical personal relationship with Jesus. Now, this is an adventure of the highest order! Jesus is the perfect source of unconventional wisdom and strength necessary to sustain you and your son. He loves you both deeply, deeply enough to conquer death for you. The challenge facing us as parents is how to make Jesus alive for our boys.

Now, I've Got Some Bad News and I've Got Some Good News

The bad news? You are raising an alien with no concept of God.

A boy has no discernible spiritual sensitivity, no yearning for higher truth. If you recall from the lessons on development, a boy has no appreciation of the abstract but instead focuses his mental energies on concrete things like people, places, and things. His faith? His faith in you? Unless shown otherwise, a boy will not have a natural spiritual awareness until his early teens.

The good news? A boy has remarkable responsiveness to spiritual things once they are introduced. He clings to spirituality with refreshing tenacity and handles it as normal and natural.

How do you teach Jesus so your boy gets Him? I suggest sharing actual events that happened in the Bible, telling your son stories, and teaching him to pray.

Share Actual Happenings in the Bible

Stick to lessons about people, places, and events. Teach history lessons, maps, miracles, and wars. A boy understands all that! And he needs it to grow. A student of the Koran remarked after reading the Bible that Christianity wasn't really a religion. The Bible, he said, was a history book!

It's a history book so alive that it would bleed if cut. We should appreciate the liveliness and relevance of the Bible. We must attain a perfect, conscious conviction of the facts in Scripture. Our sons need exposure to these literal occurrences, and they need to be related through us.

Tell Your Son Stories

You need to learn to tell stories to your son. A well-spun yarn is unforgettable. That's one reason Jesus did it so much. His teaching parables followed some very simple rules that we can all learn.

First, they were spontaneous. Jesus frequently spun parables on the spot, relying on ongoing circumstances to dictate the means of the message He taught. He seemed constantly on the lookout for moments when He could relate an ongoing experience to a truth He wanted to plant in the hearer.

Second, His stories were simple and short. For boys, this is a perfect formula. Creating long, convoluted story lines is spellbinding. For building foundations in your son, however, brevity captivates best.

Third, Jesus always used familiar threads to spin parables. Oftentimes they were not that creative, but they were experiences the listener had familiarity with: harvesting, fishing, fetching water, pruning trees, and so on. Become familiar with the world of your son, and make up stories and teaching tales based on things he does daily.

Fourth, the lessons were always creatively suggested by the story, not spelled out. Keep your tales purposely vague, and make your boy think. Letting his head "cook" on the meaning of your story is fine. After a short cook time, explain the meaning of the story you told. There's no need for extensive elaboration (a common parental plague). Just say what it meant and leave it.

If he asks you for more clarification, do as Jesus did and tell another parable! Draw your boy out with these parables, and tease his brain with the clear truths you know.

To get acquainted with telling stories, lift one from the long list that Jesus used, and say it. Read it verbatim if you must. I have personally experienced profound power in telling the story just as Jesus did. Try it.

Fifth, you can tell stories within stories. ("There was once a man who told this tale to his son . . .") Such embedding of information in a long story is powerful for relaying important information. If you carefully read Jesus' parables, you will witness a Master of this art form at work.

TEACH HIM TO PRAY

All too often prayer is the act of last (or lost) hope. We must teach our boys to practice prayer as a way of life. And we must teach them that Jesus listens to our prayers. Good prayer is a focused conversation for sharing a relationship with a living God.

Make your prayers lively conversations that your boy can be perfectly excited about. An enthusiastic prayer life is the sure sign of a living faith!

Teach your boy to pray like this:

Dear Lord,

Thank You!

Thank You that I am able to walk and talk.

Thank You that I am able to see and smell the great stuff You placed in the world around me.

Thanks for people who love me, and for those I am able to help.

Thanks, Lord, that You are always here next to me, that You're dependable, that You laugh with me and You cry with me.

Thank You, Lord, that I cannot hide from Your love and acceptance, and no matter what I do, You love me.

Make me a person like You, Lord, and build in me courage and strength.

Above all, Father, teach me how to love—especially people I don't like.

Though I don't always know what to do, show me, Father, right from wrong, and stay here to guide me in my decisions.

Now, let's have a great day!

Amen.

When He's in Doubt, Love Him

We have wisely chosen the metaphor of the Renaissance to explain the unique features that need to be built into your son. The whole issue of building faith is a bit different from the other traits. Your boy may happily skip with you down this path, then suddenly balk on issues of faith. Doubting is distinctly human. At that point, you have a choice to make.

You can tie a rope around his waist and drag him. Or you can scald him with your tongue and make the immersion in God's truth an acid bath. Or you can do what Jesus did.

Jesus had a very interesting way of dealing with people. If people came to Him in humility, He was very kind and gentle with them. If they came with haughty pride, He was devastating. When dealing with your son, please observe one caveat: *Love him first.* If you don't love your boy intensely, all your profound and impressive lessons will be lost in an ocean of misunderstanding. Love him first, and if that is all he ever can know, that's enough. The warmth of the presence of Jesus in you is a base from which he can never escape.

If you aren't in the habit of praying constantly for your boy, please begin. Think of a shaken-up can of pop cracked open quickly: Spray effervescent prayers from your lips, and let them saturate this lifelessness around us. I suspect that if this lesson is the only one you applied in this entire book, you would have done the most potent activity for genuine happiness, peace, and direction.

Boys Are Boomerangs

Remember that this is an adventure, not a tea party! Prepare yourself for some turbulence soon. It is normal for a boy to flee all the sensibilities you taught him as a youngster. Without some forewarning, you might feel frantic when it happens. Your greatest challenge will be to trust the foundation you carefully created as he sails off toward the horizon. He may keep on course. Or he may not return to his spiritual roots till his twenties, thirties, or forties, but he'll be back. Pray for it. Anticipate it. It'll happen.

If your life has come to this point with little or no crisis, count your blessings and fasten your seat belt. Child rearing inevitably involves some difficulties, confusion, and troubles. Prepare your faith for some application. You'll be rewarded.

WELL DONE, GOOD AND FAITHFUL SERVANT

If you plant Jesus in your boy, you have given him a second pulse that is new life. When trouble hits, you may wonder if all this great Renaissance training was worth a hill of beans. You may loudly question yourself and those around you: What went wrong? What have I done? Pray for strength and pray for him. Everything's gonna be all right.

If you keep your faith, someday in the distant future you will look up and see a beat-up boomerang circling overhead. He'll be looking for home and someone to patch him up and put him together. His heart will direct him home to the faith imparted to him as a child. And you will be grateful for God, who loves you, a faith that sustains you, a boy who has Jesus as his compass, and a life that was never less than a heart-thumping adventure! That's real Renaissance living.

The Millennial Generation

It was ten years ago that I first had the thought to write this book. Many changes have occurred in the meantime. Some of those changes have been good. Others have been bad. Some changes have hit us in the face and rocked our lives completely. Others have changed our lives almost imperceptibly. It's a chaotic moment in world history, on one hand scary and intimidating, and at the same interesting and exhilarating. It's full of confusion, fascination, trepidation, and electrifying opportunity.

Through it all, one thing has not changed: boys. They're identical, functionally equivalent to any boy at any time in history. They still play and think and scheme and dream. Their toys and preoccupations have changed, but the basic chassis is the same. The path to raising them to be extraordinary men has shifted a bit, but not in any way that you can't handle. The basics are identical.

Muhammad Ali said, "The person who looks at life at 50 the same way they did at 20 has wasted 30 years of their life." I've changed a lot since I first wrote this book. I've matured as a writer, thinker, and most of all as a dad. Though I still believe everything that I first wrote, experience has painted more detail into my understanding of how boys operate. Experience, when working properly, transforms people from merely smart or clever into wise and seasoned resources for others. My wish at this moment is to do my best to offer you what seasoning and wisdom I've clumsily stumbled upon in the last decade. And make no mistake, I still love boys. I really do love these little guys.

I get lots of e-mail from worried and wondering parents. I think worry and wonder are good things. They're emotions of action, urging us to find better ways to do the old things. They empower us to change and move to higher levels of living. Worry and wonder can be good things you must welcome and respond to actively.

I've spent some time combing through the questions I've received over the years to come up with the problems that most often perplex and confound parents. I'd like to spend just a little time replying to the common confusions and mysteries, and offer what step-by-step, hardheaded suggestions make sense to me now. I will make every attempt to provide some dry-cleaner crisp suggestions to the old problems that may remain wrinkly, and make every effort to offer a new suit of clothes for the new kinds of problems we must face in the twenty-first century.

For your part I would ask three simple things. *First,* read these answers with an open mind. I've become a lot more confident and controversial since I first toddled into this book-writing biz. I've explored areas of personal development that are largely unknown, and I'm very excited about the new information I have to offer you.

Second, let yourself be curious. Curiosity and the willingness to entertain new ideas are the motors of change. And you must change. You have no choice if your desire is to be effective in these tumultuous times.

Last, don't believe anything I say without first testing it out. Try these suggestions for yourself. What you *know* counts for nothing. The only thing that matters is what you can *do.* What you can do equals how far you are willing to follow these suggestions to their natural conclusion, then decide if you like what you see. Remember, this child-rearing business is messy and imprecise, full of opportunity to test and watch and learn. Embrace this fact or your parenting years will be long and difficult.

Preparing for the Next Ten Years

The future is coming. Are you ready? If you're not, get with it. The future will not be kind to those who are unprepared to grapple with it. Lots of strange things are going to happen. The disparity between the haves and have-nots will widen, the information age will spin off its version of refugees, homeless drifters, and illiterates, and potentially jeopardize everything you currently enjoy. The rules for everything will be rewritten, and you'd best get on the team that's writing them.

How do you do that? Start by doing your best to peer into the future with me. Seeing the trends is rather easy. These big trends are actually pretty obvious. What takes some genius is seeing the things that are going on right now in front of us, then taking action.

This is important because, in the span of ten years, your boy is going to traverse perhaps the most life-shaping experiences of his existence. As the saying goes, there are three kinds of people in the world: those who make things happen, those who watch things happen, and those who ask what happened. Don't be in the last group.

Encapsulating what all the smarty-pants are predicting for the next ten to twenty years of our lives is tough. Let me try to bring you up to speed. Technology has, is, and will continue to change everything. It will influence every nook and cranny of our lives. No obscure corner will be spared. Microchips will rule the world.

The changes are going to both fascinate and terrorize us. The economy will flourish, education will be provided by an ever-broadening Internet, and technology will seem no less than sorcerer's magic. Biomedical advances will allow people to stay alive practically as long as they like. Advice and information will be provided by virtual friends, powered by microchips of thundering power. Those with good jobs will learn to do things computers cannot, which will occupy an ever shrinking range of options. Life as we've known it is over.

What's the best way to adapt to this? Well, adaptation is the key word. Learn about computers and do it now. Those who are unfamiliar with technology will be a slave to it. Kids without computer skills will spend most of their days looking through the frosted windowpanes of those that have them. Encourage your kids (and be encouraged) to be proactive consumers of education, financial information, and medical services. Ask your boy for help on this if you must. In most cases he'll gladly oblige (if he can find the time).

And above all else, keep the faith. God is in control of everything, and we will never encounter anything that He did not see and for which He has not properly prepared.

Enjoy the ride!

More on Sports

I've spent some years as a professional sports consultant. I must confess that for all my past obsession with sports I spend almost no time "watching the game and having a Bud." And I like it that way. Watching sports bores me. At the risk of sounding like an old grump I really think we just watch too much and participate too little. For heaven's sake don't settle for so little. Get a life, then live it hard.

And while you're at it, encourage your boys to do the same. Many parents contact me about boys mixed up in all forms of trouble. I can tell you that across the board it's rare for me to field a question about a young athlete getting in trouble. Does it happen? Of course. But it seems that athletics is a great release of some kind for boys. It seems to have a calming effect on their combative tendencies.

Allow me to make a perfectly safe statement: Having your son involved with sports is more helpful than hurtful, and too much athletic involvement is not something you should worry about. At the risk of redundancy, boys need to burn energy to be healthy. Computerconditioned, television-tranquilized, video-game-hypnotized bodies are not good. Make your boy get outside, get air, get dirty, get sporty. It used to be when we were kids that being grounded meant being locked up in the house. Today many teens loathe the thought of being made to go outside. (Grounding kids to the outdoors works surprisingly well as discipline—try it!)

Send your boy outside. He may not like being asked to go outside; he may fuss and whine and fume. All the more reason to release him into the wilds. Make him do it, and as he goes out the door hand him a ball.

TOUGHNESS DOES NOT EQUAL HATE

The audiences I address are all different, with some interesting threads of similarity. One of those threads is the almost universal belief that to be tough on kids is somehow hateful or unkind. Too many of the parents I speak with believe that to be tough on kids somehow suggests that they don't love them.

Now if you know anything about me, you know that I try to live full-out, acting from strength and confidence rather than timidity. To that end I'd like to advocate something rather old-fashioned. I'd like to suggest that we allow ourselves to be just 10 percent tougher on our kids than we are right now. I say this because I believe that raising our children in an antiseptic, trouble-free, pain-free environment is probably one of the most damaging things we can do to them. In our niceness we're building kids who haven't the slightest clue what real life is about.

Most of us realize by now that life has a tendency to kick you in the teeth from time to time. It's heartless that way and doesn't really care how much you weep, complain, or shout foul. The problem is that many of our kids don't know life is like this until they're accomplished whiners.

Boys unfit to face this kind of world are handicapped. And they grow this way because we're afraid to release them a bit and let them experience the world as it actually is.

I think boys should experience many things. From total happiness and excess to total privation and misery. Do them a favor and expose them to the exact range that life will fire at them. Sounds harsh, but I don't know of any other way to prepare them for what they will experience along the road when your ability to help has passed. You've got an obligation to make life a little hard on them now. Miss this chance and life will deal the lessons, and let me tell you, it will be nasty.

The good news is that installing a toughness in your boys is pretty easy. I would suggest three things:

Allow him to experience some measured degree of struggle. This one is easy. You prepare kids for tough situations by exposure and experience. You can't prep for toughness with pacifiers and marshmallow parenting. I know I probably sound like a marine, but ask any older person if I'm not correct. Children of this era really don't have much of a concept of struggle or difficulty. And those are not bad things to experience. Measured toughness doesn't equal hatred of your kids.

Put him in situations where he's uncomfortable and let him figure his own way out. Stay out! Overrule your impulse to rescue little Cecil. He needs to learn to feel alone and in trouble, then decide what he's going to do about it. This is a learned human life skill, and it's not picked up on the back of a cereal box. Start simple: For example, don't always answer all his questions, but get in the habit of first saying "What do you think?" or "Is that a question you can answer for yourself?" Work your way up to asking him to figure out more difficult matters, like how he's going to afford all the new toys he wants, how he's going to deal with bullies and all those "unfair" kids at school, what he's going to do when you kick him outside to go play.

To the person immersed in the late twentieth century child-rearing doctrine or to new parents, I sound really harsh. I'm not. Keep this in mind: Life is going to kick these kids very hard. If you love them, prepare them under real situations.

Get him used to the word tough. Just say it without feeling guilt or pity. That would be a good start. When you say it, rather than dissolving into a sea of angst and fear of being hated, convince yourself that what you're doing is giving your boy a life-saving vitamin. Many of the hard things in life do end up being vitamins that make us stronger, but they don't appear that way at the start. Just say the words and walk away knowing you've done something good for your son.

And don't give in when he tries out his manipulation arsenal. He'll run through a sequence, his sequence, from innocent and flirty to harsh and guilt inducing. He doesn't care which one works, and he's programmed to simply try them all until one of them hits. Don't think his words and theatrics mean anything. They don't. They're just intended to get you to respond in his favor. Stay strong.

GRANDPARENTING

It's unnatural for grandparents to feel like frontline personnel in this battle for boys. But you are. The velocity and form with which we live our lives might lead you to believe that your wisdom, experience, and service have no place. But they do. You have a visibly important role to play in rearing your grandchildren, and they are waiting for you to act.

Grandparents have many natural roles. One is to pass on the accumulated history of your life to the next generation. You are the linchpin connecting the past with the future, and the knowledge you now possess is beneficial to future generations. Another role is that of maintaining family traditions. Yet another is casting your seasoned and wise perspective over the immediate matters of the day. Are you doing all this? If not, let me make a few suggestions:

Have confidence! I sense that decades of ignoring the wisdom of treasured people like you is giving way to a fresh new appreciation. Be prepared to render opinions about current and past events if asked. Be upbeat and optimistic; gloom-and-doom grandparents don't get asked their opinions very often. I see many moments coming in the future when others are going to come to you for your input, and you must be prepared.

Think of some good things to say! Did you know that it's possible to live many years, and have lessons, experiences, and ideas but arrive at old age with nothing to say? Don't allow this to happen to you. Until the day you die you will learn and think and develop wisdom that is special to you. Organize your vast memories and thoughts on a variety of subjects including money, love, happiness, worries, children, good times, bad times, and so on.

Make yourself available for advice! I know many grandparents who never get asked their opinion because nobody knows they are offering it. Be especially aware of this with your grandson. Give them advice freely, for you are a big shot to them. Develop opinions on boys' problems like bullies, manhood, destiny, drugs, winning, losing, and the like. Your input will be highly valued. Formulate good rationale for what you say, and speak it with authority. Your grandson is waiting for you to stand and speak. He needs to hear what you say!

This was a growing trend a decade ago that's now hitting full speed—grandparents parenting again. It causes great fear among grandparents, but let me assure you that grandparents have way more going for them than they believe.

I'm actually surprised by how many grandparents show up at my events. They're typically there for one of two reasons: (1) Their grandbaby (no matter how old he is) is giving them fits and they've lost their confidence (2) Grandma and Grandpa are fighting about the best way to handle things. Let's deal with each.

Let me say again that boys are just like the good ole days. What worked before will work now, with one important difference: Boys today are *not* used to the level of respect required of you when you were a kid. That's my generation's fault. Please accept my apologies. It takes them a bit to adjust, but they can adjust to anything required of them. Boys are *very* adaptable. Like your grandchild's first generation should've done, set some rules, your rules, and stick by them. Your old parenting skills are just like old tools: They work fine even though they don't look like much.

I like to see grandparents cooperating on this parenting-again thing. But that is often not the case. If you're in a contentious situation with your kid over the grandkids, negotiate, but don't sell out. If you're going to parent, you must do it on your terms or you're going to go gray, so to speak. As I see it, he who has the kid sets the rules. So listen to the input of your grandchild's parents, but you set the rules. It is one right you should never relinquish.

Now, about grandparenting wars. Nothing is harder to address than the low-level, intense, and stubborn fights I sometimes see between grandparents. Personally I hate to see this, not because I hate fights (which I do), but because they often have the feel of loggerheads that won't yield. It would seem that wisdom would make people more supple, but this kid thing can bring out the worst in what lies deeply buried in old relationships.

Allow me to state what is obvious to those on the outside: A house divided cannot stand. This section cannot provide marriage counseling, but I would suggest you get some if your civil war is affecting your ability to be unified and work together. Raising grandkids is not something you probably planned on, so the stresses can be surprising and powerful. Seeking help in these times, should you need it, is a sign of strength.

Remember that the most important attribute you bring to your grandchild is stability and predictability. So do your best to aim your efforts at creating stability, a unified front, an ability to work through problems together, and a willingness to be wrong—all qualities of a well-oiled relationship.

And don't underestimate your influence. Kids are notoriously poor at speaking about what they feel, and though they feel deeply attached and grateful to you, they'll hardly ever say so. Don't take silence on this to mean anything. You mean the world to them though they'll never say so.

MOMS RAISING BOYS SOLO

Okay, Mom, let's talk. This is not nearly as big a deal as you might have been led to believe. With all the input we're hearing, confusion on this topic is the only thing that's clear. Let's defog.

Boys need men as they get older. All women know that. You can mother too much. All mothers know that. Sometimes the best you can do is imperfect. All solo moms know that very well. And like all kids, they all somehow survive trauma and difficulty, and for the most part end up just fine. Many mothers don't know this!

Let me make several suggestions. As I've mentioned in other parts of this book, I know many men who were raised by single moms and have turned out to be the finest guys you'd ever meet. Obviously, something else is at work here that you need to know about. In my mind it boils down to several things. *First,* solo mothers of successful boys choose a course of action and have confidence about themselves. Think about what you want to do with your son, then believe in it. When solo moms show confidence, it seems to have a winning effect on boys.

Second is something you probably already know: Boys need men at some point. Men interact with boys in a completely different way from women. Boys need this sort of interaction to be healthy. Men know how to get boys tough, and I believe they need that. Well-adjusted boys are not girls, and it takes a man to help shape that facet of his personality.

If a man's available, encourage his participation (which you probably do). The big problem is if no man is around. This is not a death sentence for your son. Try these tactics: (1) Forget the past and the guilt that most certainly haunt you. Move on and deal with a life whose most challenging aspects are coming at you frontally. The past only lives to the extent that you keep it on life support. (2) Be 25 percent harder on your son than you might be normally. Roughhouse with him, be physical and play hard. (3) Encourage him to express his emotions *without* whining, pouting, or crying. Those tactics are for children, not adults. Warmth and motherly kindness are fine, but toss in some icy coolness. No apologies. No smiles. The reason is that men give boys that harder-edged form of interaction, and boys need it. Though it may violate your instincts, gulp hard and don't "mother" him.

Last, help your son surmount what might be his fear of men. What boys respect they fear. Respect and fear are good. I know that might sound crazy, but let's not be intentionally ignorant or sappy about this: Fear is a huge part of what motivates us to good, and to that end let's not squelch it. Just because something (fear) sounds bad doesn't make it bad. Don't let the current definitions of good and bad parenting (which are notoriously fickle and dogged by withering stupidity) erode your real street smarts. Help your son deal with his natural fear of men in a heads-up, informed way.

Here's how: Expose him to some men that he might like. You might have to be real assertive in setting up this sort of interaction, but it's important. See to it that your boy has the chance for at least some passing interaction with an adult male. Do it at church, social clubs, sports events, extracurricular school events, etc. There are men all around, and trust me, if you share with them your desire to get your son in the presence of a good strong man, well, flattery gets you everywhere. Men instinctively understand what you mean and will find it hard to turn their back on your boy.

TEACHERS

You are big juicy pieces of the "grand scheme of things" pie. Yet I wonder if our society isn't eating you alive. I'd like to take a few moments to affirm your life-giving contributions and suggest how we may all win this battle together.

You decided to enter this wonderful profession for many reasons. One of those reasons was to educate kids and impart information to others. This desire is one of your natural-born gifts, and you would practice whether or not you were in a classroom. You spend more time with some kids than their parents do, and you deserve special thanks and some encouragement.

Teaching can be thankless. Does it seem as though many parents aren't playing on your team? Does it seem that there's never enough money to buy what you need to teach well? Does it seem that the administration just doesn't understand your problems? Aren't the press and politicians a little harsh in blaming you for failing kids? All these factors combine with others to make your already difficult job much tougher.

Let me help. Education is a people business, and despite all the hoopla about new generations, people don't change that much. Parents will always range from careless to hyperinvolved: penny-pinching administrators will always squeeze, and people will always blame others for embarrassing problems or the lackluster performance of kids. Remember, they made Socrates drink hemlock two thousand five hundred years ago for improper teaching! People don't change.

The fact that these situations are unchanging doesn't mean you should surrender. There are many things you can control, and in all candor they're the most important elements anyway. You must focus on the winnable battles and fight them with courage and enthusiasm. One of those winnable battles is fought squarely in the hearts of your kids.

Children's lives depend on their teachers. You occupy an enormous, hallowed space within their world. Twenty-five years from now, when all your teachings have long since become thoughtless habits to your students, they will remember you. How you looked, how you acted, your enthusiasm, if you liked them or if you even cared. That's what they will remember. And you can control those things.

What can I tell you about boys that you don't already know? Probably very little. As you have no doubt noticed about this book, my attitude is that boys are quite understandable. What's lacking is the nerve, excitement, and creativity we need in solving the problems we face with boys.

You will recall that my purpose in writing this book is not to fix broken boys. My goal is to help parents to accept responsibility of this challenge and equip them with some ideas and techniques that work.

My challenge to you is similar. I won't ask you to become Teacher of the Year. I won't ask you to pack more into an already cramped and busy schedule. I will, however, ask you to monitor and assume responsibility for three areas: your attitude toward your boy; the level at which you expect him to perform; and the energy level and attitude with which your boy attacks his education.

1. If I've learned anything in consulting with sports teams, it's that a team reflects the unconscious beliefs of its coach. This can be observed in all team sports, business, families, or otherwise. *Your beliefs about what your boys can do constitute the limit of what you will let them do.* Anything they accomplish above and beyond your beliefs is simply because they ignored you and went ahead.

Your beliefs matter. I've been told by teachers that as a general rule, girls are more cooperative, teachable, and manageable than boys. It's easy to be excited and enthusiastic about those qualities. Boys are generally more trying. A teacher's discouragement might seem logical in the face of a boy's apparent stupidity and ignorance, his sometimes surly and uncooperative dispositions, and his silly little ego. Still you must believe good, big things for your boys in spite of all this.

2. Closely linked to your beliefs about your boys are your expectations about their level of performance. With all your teaching experience, you needn't be with a boy long to get a "read" on him. You can tell what kind of kid he is in about five minutes! You can swiftly form a fairly accurate feel for his potentials and abilities. But beware: I have personally made swift judgments about boys that turned out to be incorrect, inadvertently crushing perfectly good potential.

Boys know very well what you think of them. You can't hide it. For good measure, always set your expectations of your boys higher than you really think they can reach. Not way higher, just ever so slightly higher. It might be a stretch for them to live up to your expectations, but a healthy and helpful stretch.

3. You are a major motivator in the life of every boy you know. Think about this: Boys think of you as the person they must perform for. This is a belief present in their minds before you say or do anything. What a terrific psychological force in the lives of your boys if you use this influence.

How do you motivate your boys to learn on their own? Notice that motivation to learn is as natural as the motivation to eat. Your job is not to motivate learning but to lay out good things to eat. Teachers are cooks!

The motivation to learn is normally distributed in the population of boys. That means some boys are more driven than others. You can't force-feed those lacking an appetite, but you can faithfully keep the meals coming, never losing your taste for the good stuff. All your boys will find something to eat if you keep it up.

Guard your attitude and keep it positive and upbeat. This establishes a powerful, permeating expectation for success. Your optimism and energetic outlook will excite and stimulate your boys. Expect a lot, and push them as hard as you are able.

Let me leave you with some parting thoughts. If you can change the way you see a situation, the force of that vision will automatically change the way you act in that situation. If you can see the opportunity to teach with authority, confidence, enthusiasm, and commitment to a purpose, you will change and your kids will see your classroom situation differently. It's like sales: The person most energized and eager about the product will excite others and make sales. Making a sale becomes simply a question of how you view the opportunity and the enthusiasm you provide.

But in sales you don't always make the sale. You don't get many pats on the back, either! Too many parents throw a thankless "educate my kid" mantle on you. You would probably rather not wear it alone, but you have no choice. We all know that education starts at home, but too often it just doesn't happen. Perhaps this situation will change, but for now we must take courage and gather our wits to give these kids the best we have to offer.

ADHD

Actually, this diagnosis causes more ADHD among parents than the kids! In reality ADHD is a difficult diagnosis to make, so you should take care in understanding it as much as you can. The Diagnostic and Statistical Manual of Mental Disorders IV suggests that ADD comes in three flavors:

1. Attention-Deficit/Hyperactivity Disorder (which is, by the way, why "ADHD" is sometimes referred to as "ADD"; the acronyms can be used interchangeably), Combined type. This describes a child who is deemed both hyperactive and inattentive.

2. Attention-Deficit/Hyperactivity Disorder, Predominantly Inattentive type. This describes the child deemed inattentive without hyperactivity.

3. Attention-Deficit/Hyperactivity Disorder, Predominantly Hyperactive-Impulsive type. This describes the child deemed hyperactive and impulsive without severe inattention.

To make the diagnosis of ADHD, a full psychological workup must be completed by a competent professional. That can be pricey, but well worth it if you suspect your boy labors under the yoke of this problem. It is especially important if you're going to begin the process of evaluating your son for drug therapy.

Let me make a suggestion here if you can't afford a $500 evaluation. When in doubt, ask a teacher. These professionals see many kinds of kids across a broad spectrum of situations, and much weight should be given to their opinion. They are often a great source of advice about whether or not your kid is ADHD, and if you're wondering, ask them to judge your kid as a percentage of all the kids they've ever seen (e.g., "he would fall in the upper 80 percent of the kids I've ever seen"). Though it's not scientific, very little of psychology is rigorously scientific anyway. A qualified teacher's opinion will often closely overlap what most professional evaluations suggest.

The real value of professional involvement is to advise you on treatment options. But buyer beware: Professionals tend to suggest treatments of their profession. If you talk to a hammer salesman he's going to suggest hammers. Psychiatrists believe in drugs and medical centers. Psychologists believe in testing and talking. Social workers want to adjust family dynamics. Hammer salesmen believe in ball-peens.

So whom should you trust? Well, all kidding aside, you should get the input of many people. I do believe in drugs by the way. I've seen them do miracles. But first I'd try several things. Diet control should be one of your first adjustments. It would seem obvious to control sugar intake, but many parents are oblivious to what their kids are doing. Make sure meals are balanced, regular, and that you limit junk food consumption. Consult an experienced, or better yet *recommended* dietician for more details. Make sure to befriend your local health food store guru, as their input can be both fascinating and on the whole pretty harmless if they're wrong.

Last, examine yourself. Make sure that if you're taking medical action on this ADHD business that it's for the right reasons. If you're doing it because little Eddy's just being a normal monster, maybe that's not a good enough reason to use medication. Make sure you're doing it for his own good and not just exclusively your own.

In the future, science will perfect mood control drugs. That's a very safe bet. Whether that's good or not is too early to say. If I had a truly ADHD son, I'd be first in line for help. But be cautious—ask lots of questions and interact with professionals who are on the cutting edge of this fast-changing technology. The Internet is a great way to do this, and other parents of ADHD kids can be a valuable source of uncommon information as well.

FYI, the teen years seem to burn out this ADHD problem. Puberty starts internal chemical changes that alter the effect of ADHD. Your son will grow up and grow out of this. So, if you can just hold on, the chemical cavalry is coming!

ALCOHOL, TOBACCO, AND FIREARMS

I guess the world has changed a bit if we feel the need to discuss these things with our boys. Let's not hesitate.

School-based alcohol/drug abuse programs such as DARE are doing a remarkable job of putting alcohol and drug abuse prevention right under our kids' noses. They learn the drill, and statistics show that it works better than many things. But I think all DARE leaders would heartily agree that real alcohol and drug abuse prevention "starts at home." As I've asked around, I've discovered that many parents don't know what that means. It means you talk to your boy about abstaining from alcohol and drugs, and make open communication about these topics normal and regular. Even for young boys, these problems are real, so you might as well get them used to conversing about it early.

Same with tobacco. And in addition, remember some kindergarten wisdom: monkey see, monkey do. If anything defines a youthful mind, it's curiosity. Drink and smoke in the presence of your boys, and guess what happens? This is a no-brainer.

Now, guns. Let me start by saying I believe in guns. I like guns. They're important. But you've got to respect them and treat them in a systematic, disciplined way. Guns aren't going away, and chances are good that whether you like it or not, your boy is going to encounter one either accidentally or otherwise. Let's teach our boys about them.

Gun safety classes are a must. Find an NRA certified instructor (a gun shop in your town will help you) and tell them I sent you. Tell them you wish to have your son be exposed to handguns and shouldered weapons, and learn how to handle them properly. Without fail, attend these classes with your boy.

COMPUTERS AND THINGS ELECTRONIC

There is a lot to be said about this, but again the basics can be sifted out easily. Since I first wrote this book, computers have taken on entirely new dimensions in our lives. People need to be computer literate, and that need is only going to grow. Kids must know about computers and electronic devices without allowing themselves and their lives to be controlled by them. Herein lies the danger.

I've long advocated having a life. That means not being an observer of what's going on but being actively involved. The problem with the way many kids interact with computers is that they're being reduced to observers and slaves. Their attention and energy are being gobbled up by an inanimate machine that has an ever-increasing ability to control them.

To overcome this I would suggest several things. *First,* apply limits to the time your kids spend with electronic gadgets and by all means tie their use of machines to some sort of physical output. Like television, suggest for example that they spend an hour outside playing for every two hours of computer use. Use a timer if you must. Don't worry if you don't hit that mark precisely, but keep in mind that the real objective here is to make your son well-rounded and active, not just passive and semicomatose. Yes, I know computers engage the brain and that's good. But an equal involvement of the body is just as, if not more, important at this stage in life.

Second, supervise what's going on. It's called "parental controls," and I would advocate not merely allowing your service provider to decide what parental controls are. It used to be asked, "Do you know where your kids are?" but I would suggest that you apply the same style of supervision to "Do you know what your kids are doing on-line?"

If you don't know, you can follow several electronic footprints to find out what your kids are doing. Consult your computer manual about finding cookie folders, history folders, and Internet temp files to find out what Internet sites have been visited by the user of the machine. There are also software packages commercially available that allow you to monitor what's up. I strongly advocate using these.

I would be especially alert about Internet gaming. Kids today can play thousands of "real time" games with other players anywhere in the world, right from the quiet of their own computer. These games can range from chess to some of the most violent and bloody simulation games you can imagine. They're fun and fast-paced—the perfect recipe for capturing young minds.

I'm not going to tell you what's right for your boy, but I am going to suggest that his involvement in these games can be a significant time consumer, and it's up to you to decide if it's appropriate. And Internet simulation games are only going to grow, so read and learn all you can about it now.

While you're at it, e-mail your kids. I've heard many stories of people who have e-mail conversations with kids right in their own homes. It may sound strange but it works. Kids can often open up on-line in ways more honest and genuine than if you approached them directly.

It's in the DNA: What the Human Genome Tells Us

Since this book was originally published, the entire human genome (the sequence of genes that create human beings) has been mapped. Geneticists have learned some fascinating things in the process. Among those findings is that 75 percent of genetic material has no apparent use. We share 99.99 percent identical genetic mapping. We're 99 percent identical to apes (especially teenage boys I think). And finally, environment plays a far larger role in determining who we are than genes.

There's good news and bad news here. First the good news. I recently saw a segment on a morning news show that showed two pigs that had been cloned. Genetically they were identical, yet the two piggly wigglies couldn't have appeared more different. One was fat and squirmy, the other thin and quiet, yet genetic copies.

How can this be? As the researcher pointed out, making you who you are is much more than amino acids and peptide bonds. Genetics is a complex and dizzying interplay of chromosomes and life.

Now the bad news. We are going to be facing a world where genetic engineering is an eye-popping reality, and we're going to face it soon. Frankly it all frightens me a bit, even though the vast amount of what science will be able to do will be good and beneficial to all mankind. What worries me is that I'm not sure any of us are wise enough to know what to do with all this. There are developments now in progress that will make cloning seem as harmless as cooking a cheeseburger, such things as biological-mechanical interfaces, robotics, micro machines called "nanobots," and more.

We're creating the world that our kids are going to inherit. We need to begin to be vigilant to get our kids thinking about how they intend to handle all this. To prepare them, it's wise to prepare yourself. Engage your boy with information and questions. Get him thinking about it now. If I were you, I wouldn't be content to let him drift off into this uncertain future without at least a passing knowledge of the opportunities and dangers inherent in the technology we're developing.

The interesting point here is that understanding and wisdom are not genetic traits, but are earned through thought and debate and experience. It's never too early to begin those lessons.

MORE IDEAS ON DISCIPLINE— ESPECIALLY SPANKING

When I first wrote this book, I believed deeply in the power of corporal punishment, but I was afraid to say it. I was afraid people would get arrested. Well, I'm still afraid of people getting arrested, but I'm more sure of myself these days. So let me tell you what I think.

Boys have a simple system of behavior. The system is this: Push until you're stopped. That's it! *That's their whole system of behavior.* And when they do get stopped, they just invoke the rule again: "Push until you're stopped." And when they get stopped again, they push until . . .

Get the idea? It's the utter simplicity of this that makes it somewhat hard to beat.

With that as background, let's talk a little bit about spanking and other forms of discipline. Most parents don't have a "system" anywhere near the sophistication of their kids. That's why we as parents seem to spend so much time reacting. That's exactly what we're doing. This reacting all the time has a tendency to make adults cranky, especially if you're the kind of parent who's overly tolerant, then bursts at the seams when pushed just a little too far.

I think there's a better way, and it plays into the hands of spanking . . . no pun intended. Boys need warnings that they're approaching a "no-fly" zone, and they need swift and unapologetic predictability when they cross the line. Actually, you'll find that well-behaved kids all share one trait: They believe their parents. They believe that if their parents say something bad will happen if they act up, something bad will happen.

As a rule, misbehaved kids are the opposite. They think that if they misbehave they'll be able to weasel out somehow. That's why I believe that all discipline should be oriented toward establishing your credibility. Spanking, if done properly, has the profound ability to make boys believe that what you say, you mean. "Properly" means issuing a prior warning (one), with specific detail about when and where and how much spanking will occur and within what time frame if certain behavior does not stop. Then with absolute, total, irrevocable, undeniable, unbendable, unappeasable certainty, *do exactly what you say you'll do!*

Will it harm your kids? Beating your kids will harm them, spanking will not. The difference is enormous. Beating is out of anger, uncontrolled, often without warning, sometimes using weapons. Spanking is planned, warned, never used with weapons or devices, and is tightly controlled. As a rule I'd suggest 2 swats on the butt at 2 lbs. of pressure at a 90 degree bending position. Increase up to 3 swats as needed. If this fails to get a response, do it differently, at your discretion.

If spanking is completely repugnant to you, well, all right. At least put some sort of system in place. I advocate the Smart Discipline System of Dr. Larry Koenig, Ph.D. (*Smart Discipline: Fast, Lasting Solutions for Your Peace of Mind and Your Child's Self-Esteem,* Harper Resources, 2002). It's a simple system with a great track record of success.

And let me add one more thing. Remember that an ancillary facet of the discipline diamond is building a relationship with your son. I never thought it was smart (or very nice) to spank a child you didn't love and spend some time with. It works much better not as an expedient means of changing behavior, but as a means to establish something between a parent and a child. If you're going to spank, spend some time with them. It's the right thing to do.

THE ULTIMATE SELF-ESTEEM: CONFIDENCE AND SKILL

Self-esteem has become such a sacred cow in our country. Fire up the barbecue.

The reason I rail so hard against self-esteem, in addition to the fact that it all sounds so self-serving, is that it doesn't square with anything I've ever learned about excellence. Greatness comes from sacrificing yourself, not loving yourself. To be honest, folks, this is old news. The Homeric poets were writing about that four thousand years ago, but somehow the lesson got lost amid our steady desire to placate and tease our children into goodness. Call me a marine, but I think self-sacrifice, self-discipline, self-control, pushing your known limits, and other basically spartan measures are a superior way to live. Semper Fi.

You will serve your son best if you focus not on verbalizing how great thou art, but on helping your son demonstrate his confidence and his skill to himself. Boys know where they're at in the pecking order of their lives, and few things match the "self-esteem" building potential inherent in proving something to themselves. Especially if it will help them improve their ranking or give them some sort of bragging rights. Boys need that, and it's good.

Pursuits that build a boy's sense of self-confidence and self-respect include sports achievements, hobbies (especially unusual ones), adventures that are successfully completed, scary situations conquered, new friends made, new knowledge mastered, something difficult achieved, skills or abilities discovered, etc. Any of these hold the promise of building the best kind of self-esteem around: self-respect.

THE DANGER OF ALL BEING ALIKE

I consider the author Michael Crichton to be one of our most reliable bellwethers concerning science and technology trends that will be influencing our lives in the future. He's a reliable and shrewd observer of things that should be of concern to us. In commenting on his book *Jurassic Park*, he lays out an idea I think we'd all be wise to consider. In his conversation about the nature of evolution, he goes into some detail about the dangers of the earthly "system" becoming too much alike. He asserts what is a well-known and widely accepted concept— that alikeness is dangerous. The systems that survive are those with variability. Variability brings versatility and survivability.

Which brings me to my concern. I've been watching the Internet with some keen interest, and I've witnessed a trend that bothers me. I've noticed that a joke no longer takes months to cross the country but can be spread in an hour. I've noticed that whenever anyone has an opinion, it's suddenly everyone's opinion in minutes. I've seen that there is less and less original thinking and massively more cloned thinking going on. Originality is gone. Gobbling up the ideas of everyone else and regurgitating them is in.

The problem I see is that boys are not being encouraged to be independent, flexible thinkers but rather cookies cut out of identical molds. We must be careful to train our boys about the value and good sense of being different from everyone else.

I have always been deeply intrigued by Jesus' comment in Matthew 11:12 when He said, "The Kingdom of heaven suffers violence, and the violent take it by force." What was He talking about? I think what He was saying that was the world is the playground of the action takers, the thinkers, and we'd best be among them. And we'd best teach our boys to do likewise.

Reread chapter 3 on unconventional parenting and dedicate yourself to training your son over the long haul to insist on being different from the rest of the crowd, to be an original. Get him comfortable in the role of standing up for what he reasons to be the right things, and get him used to going against the grain if integrity demands it. This is hard for boys to learn, but encouragement from you goes a long way. Be an original. Survival might depend on it.

TEACH YOUR BOY TO ASK QUESTIONS

When my boys were young, I tried my best to expose them to unusual things. People, places, challenges—I was always heads up for opportunities to put them on the firing line somehow with experiences that would push them, challenge them.

And we met a lot of interesting folks along the way. I always took the time to suggest that the boys come up with some questions to ask these people. They had no problem thinking up some simple questions once they were prompted. The boys never failed to surprise me with some of the things they asked. And to this day they've continued on their merry way, interacting with strangers with uncanny ease.

You'll find that kids in general, and boys specifically, can rise to nearly any challenge you set before them. Their talents, often latent and unseen, can bubble up with only the slightest coaxing. But you must coax and suggest and tease them out on this. They won't typically just do it on their own.

Earlier I delved into the future and discussed a little bit about what we need to do to prepare for those times. One of the most important things I think you can prepare your son for is the absolute necessity of good people skills. In most cases that boils down to a good attitude about others, generosity, and the ability to communicate well. Asking questions is, in my opinion, one of the most powerful people skills you can encourage.

Start simply. Encourage your son to simply nurture a questioning attitude about things. This questioning attitude has many spin-off benefits that will aid him in his education, his range of interests, his desire to be resourceful and seek out answers on his own, and most of all his ability to take focused interest in others ("others-esteem" I think we'll call it).

Encourage him to question everything. Why you eat dinner at six, why toilet paper is cut into squares, why plants grow up, why men have beards, why you have to be in bed at nine. You get the idea. Ask, ask, ask. It may take some time, but he'll warm up to the exercise, much to his own benefit.

MONEY AND ENTREPRENEURSHIP

I read a wonderful book that deeply affected my thinking. It's called *Rich Dad, Poor Dad* by Robert Kiasaki. In the book Kiasaki describes his own father, director of the State of Hawaii Department of Education and a Ph.D. smart-guy, but chronically broke. His other dad was a high school dropout, the father of his best friend, but he was a fantastic business success—wealthy, happy, and influential. The book compares what he learned about money from both his "dads."

This book really opened my eyes to what we need to teach our kids about America's economy. Entreprenuership will always be a hot area, and the skills for succeeding in our country's style of economics is important. Getting it requires a certain mind-set and a strong work ethic. Both of these you can pass along to your boy.

Many kids do think money grows on trees. The way you help them realize the limitations of this thinking is to teach them about economics. It's some of the best training you can provide. Give them allowances or opportunities to make money, then let them manage their own accounts. Let them buy what they need, and encourage them to know the difference between a liability and an asset. Help them learn through firsthand experience that wealth is built by creating or collecting assets and not liabilities. Checkout www.berniebucks.com for a great tutorial on these topics.

You may think such lessons are not realistic. Let me tell you what's not realistic: being broke and inadvertently teaching your kids how to get broke too. Start the lessons of business building early, encourage new ideas and business creation as early as possible. Frankly, these are some of the most fun and stimulating activities you can do with your son. And they are lessons he'll take with him.

BULLIES, HERDS, AND PECKING ORDERS

This problem has gained serious prominence over the last several years, and for good reason. Bullying is something that's been around for a long time, but victims are beginning to take vigilante-style action in some very dangerous ways. Bullies typically need to dominate peers, are loners, have little sense of remorse, and are above average in their normal aggression patterns.

Several nonverbal signs indicate that perhaps your son is being bullied. They include being afraid to walk to school, taking a different route home from school, refusing to go on the bus, begging to be driven to school, coming home with torn clothes, suddenly fearful of school, coming home hungry (some bullies steal lunch and/or money), and perhaps beginning to bully peers or siblings themselves.

Some suggestions for handling bullies include:

1. Bullies are most powerful when they can single out their victims. The solution is to have your child stay with another child at all times.

2. Bullies rely on secrecy and intimidation. Encourage your son to go to an adult immediately if threatened by a bully. This can be hard, especially if the bully is taunting or laughing at you. If necessary, encourage your child to go to a school official in private.

3. Try not to get upset. Try to keep your emotions in check. Angry outbursts and crying tend to egg bullies on.

4. Teach your child to be a "broken record." Have them preplan a phrase they'll use over and over, such as "I have to go now . . . that's what you think, but I have to go now . . ."

Many of these techniques will be helpful in reducing the chances that your son will be harassed by a bully. Obviously, in some cases you'll have to intervene and call the other child's parent or in some other way become involved. If that becomes necessary, go directly to the parent of the other child and calmly explain what's going on, and ask that they help put an end to it.

MILITARY SCHOOL

On occasion I'm asked for recommendations about "military school." That phrase is actually a throwback to when we were young and isn't really used much anymore, yet the concept is still vigorous. These are facilities designed with special staff and techniques to instill discipline in kids (most often boys).

I have heard mixed stories about the success of these sorts of institutions. I think they work best for juvenile cases, but for younger boys I would imagine that sending your son to one of these places for therapeutic reasons would be a last resort. Yet I'm practical, and I don't like to dismiss anything that has the appearance of value without first checking it out.

I'd suggest that if you think your son needs one of these institutional placements, check it out. You might be right, but you'd better convince yourself thoroughly and be absolutely sure it's the right thing before you commit. Ask lots of questions and get referrals. It's your kid's life we're talking about here. Prudence pays.

BOYS AND WAR

At this writing, our country is at war with terrorists. Our president has warned us over and over that this war will go on for a long time, and it will be unlike any war this country has ever faced. We should be prepared to talk to our boys about all of this. They'll have some questions.

Our boys really want to know three things: (1) What's going on? (2) What's going to happen next? and (3) Are they and those they love safe? Answering these questions is rather easy and straightforward. Keep it simple but be honest, clear, and reassuring—and as comforting as possible. That's all they really want.

The bigger task is that the answers need to be repeated over and over and over. Don't think your suggestion that "everything is all right" is going to remain strong when every day he sees pictures of terrorists, anthrax scares, and military police around airports. He'll question these things and need constant reassurance. Remember, his memory is short, and he tends to believe only that which he can get his hands on right now.

Acknowledgments

There are a few people without whose efforts *Boys!* would still be random chemicals scattered around my neutrons. First and foremost is my editor and friend, Victor Oliver. He saw some things here not seen by a hundred other publishers. Thank you, Vic.

I would also like to thank the entire staff of Thomas Nelson, especially Senior Editor Lila Empson and Brian Hampton and Rose Marie Sroufe. These people possess the gift of molding the prose of a hacker like me into real stuff! I'm ever grateful for their time and professionalism, and for the simple kindness of never having laughed at me!

And of course, all those on my A team. Special thanks to my co-producers, Milane and Bill. If I wanted to be Michael the Archangel, they would tell me I could do it. To Dan Schaefer, thanks for being my buddy and loyal protagonist. To Frank Redmond, Mark Montgomery, and all the other Men of the Titanic: You guys have no peers. Thanks as well to Ken Brakefield and Ken Cunning for helping identify the real enemy.

To my wonderful brood, Jacob, Jessie, and Zac: Thanks for patiently enduring my questions, my intrusions, and my ignorance. Forgive me for all those times I missed dinner to complete a chapter, and all those times I blanked out following some wild thought. In seventy-five years, when you totter around on canes and talk with no teeth, remember how much I love you. You're the most wonderful gifts God could ever have given a dad like me.

And to Kathi. When I lay bleeding and broken on this side of the road of life, you could have walked on. It would've been easy. But you chose to do something more difficult. All I remember is seeing you coming to me, bending low and whispering in my ear, "Yes, yes, you can . . . God bless you."

About the Author

Bill Beausay is a one-of-a-kind writer and speaker. As former vice president of the Academy of Sports Psychology, Bill gained an international reputation for developing athletic talent and stretching human ability through visionary programs. He has written five bestselling books, including *Girls! Helping Your Little Girl Become an Extraordinary Woman* and *Teenage Boys! Surviving and Enjoying These Extraordinary Years*. As the founder of Street Smart, a motivational ministry for teenagers and their parents, Bill speaks on hundreds of television and radio programs every year.

If you would like more information on Bill's books, tapes, and seminars, please contact him at:

Bill Beausay
P.O. Box 78383
Baton Rouge, LA 70837

phone: 225-262-6229
e-mail: bill@beausay.com
webpage: www.beausay.com